THE KNIGHTS TEMPLAR
AND IRELAND

The Knights Templar and Ireland

MICHAEL J. CARROLL

BANTRY STUDIO PUBLICATIONS

ACKNOWLEDGMENTS

I wish to acknowledge all the authors of many generations whose works I have consulted in preparing this volume. The main references are listed individually at the end of the book. Particular thanks to my son Michael and to Dick Richards for research and assistance. Also, my thanks to Noel O'Mahony of Bantry library and Tim Cadogan of Cork County Library for sourcing rare material for me.

Thanks to the following organisations for the use of images:
Société de l'Histoire et du Patrimoine de l'Ordre de Malte,
The Bridgeman Art Library, The British Library,
Bibliotheque Nationale and The Frans Hals Museum, Haarlem
Every effort has been made to contact copyright holders.
Any omissions will be rectified in future editions.

Published by Michael J. Carroll, Bantry, Co. Cork. Ireland

bantrydesigns@iol.ie

First published in 2006

Dedicated to my late father John J. Carroll

British Library Cataloguing in Publication data
Michael J. Carroll
The Knights Templar and Ireland
Ireland: Irish History.

ISBN:
0 9552039 0 2 Paperback
978 0 9552039 0 9 Paperback
0 9552039 1 0 Hardback
978 0 9552039 1 6 Hardback

Cover design by John McGillivray
Cover image and pen and wash drawings by Alan Langford
Printed in Spain by GraphyCems

CONTENTS

LIST OF ILLUSTRATIONS

PREFACE

Details concerning the Knights Templar in Ireland are extremely scarce. The names and locations of their various foundations have been hidden in the mists of time. With the exception of Scotland nowhere else has the history of the Templars been so shrouded in obscurity. The period of their limited existence in Ireland was almost completely ignored by Catholic writers and historians. Those who did mention the Templars briefly, like Harris, Archdall, Thomas d'Arcy McGee, Litton Falkiner and a few others, left the subject in utter confusion mainly due to the fact that they could not distinguish between the Knights of the Temple and the Knights of Saint John (Hospitallers).

Some erroneous accounts have the Templars fighting against the native Irish chieftains but it was the Hospitallers who engaged the Irish out of fear of losing their lands and possessions to the Crown. Besides being bound by the three vows of monastic life the Templars were bound by their Rules not to fight against, wound or kill any Christian under pain of being expelled from the Order.

In this work, I have endeavored to correct any confusion and to detail all the known facts about this unusual religious and military Order that came to Ireland in the twelfth century.

Having encountered these warrior monks or monastic-military orders in research for a number of my previous works I deemed it necessary to gather all the information possible on the brief history of their existence in Ireland. Unfortunately, they left almost nothing in documented evidence themselves and their history and activities are gleaned from the records of other religious orders and English historical sources including those of the English Crown. All of these are listed in the bibliography for those who wish to carry out further research on the subject.

Avoiding questionable sources I have tried to bring together the Templar history with special emphasis on their activities in Ireland where they were subservient to the master (prior) of the Temple in London. In all, they were active in Ireland for approximately 150 years.

The demise of this fighting Order was one of the greatest tragedies of the Middle Ages. Having given their lives fighting the Muslims in the Middle East they were rewarded by the pope and the European kings of that period by being accused of being heretics, magicians, idolaters and guilty of gross indecencies. They were to be the scapegoats for the failure of the Christian West to liberate Jerusalem and the Holy Land from the Muslims and the victims of the ongoing disputes between the papacy and the European princes especially the kings of France. Yet, the Templars tarnished their own image by becoming advisors to the kings and nobility, owners of vast tracts of land, collectors of taxes, treasurers to the kings, bankers for the nobility and the gatherers of much wealth. Many of them were eventually imprisoned, tortured and burnt at the stake.

Many books have been written about the Knights Templar since the suppression of the Order. Some deal with their exploits in other European countries and the Middle East, others are critical analyses of their trials and the demise of the Order, while many are pure fiction based on questionable 'historical facts'.

This work will be found to be of importance to those who are interested in history, involved in medieval studies and to the general public who wish to increase their knowledge of the Templars.

CHRONOLOGY

1099   The First Crusade captures Jerusalem

1113   The Order of the Hospital recognised by the Pope

1118   Formation of the Knights Templar

1128   Hugh de Payens, first Grand Master, arrives in England and Scotland

1129   Council of Troyes – Establishment of the Latin Rules for Templars

1130c Establishment of the 'Old Temple' in London

1131   Death of Hugh de Payens, the Grand Master

1130   Papal Bull, *Omne Datum Optimum*

1146   Foundation of the Templar House in Paris

1148   Second Crusade

1149   Templars granted Gaza

1160   Additional Clauses to Templar Rule

1161   Old Temple in London replaced by the 'New Temple'

1187   Christian forces defeated at Battle of Hattin

1189   Third Crusade

1190   Foundation of the Teutonic Knights

1191   Acre established as the Templar base in the Holy Land

1202   Fourth Crusade

1218   Siege of Damietta, Egypt

1221   Fifth Crusade retreats from Egypt

1229   The return of Jerusalem is negotiated by Frederick II

1224   Jerusalem taken by the Khoresmians

1248   Crusade of Saint Louis commences

1291   Christian forces driven out of Syria and Palestine by Mamaluks
       Fall of Acre and the evacuation of Holy Land

1307   Arrest of the Templars in France

1310   Peter of Bologna and Reginald of Provins defend Templars

1311   Council of Vienne, France

1312   Suppression of the Templars
       Transfer of properties to Hospitallers

1313   James de Molay, Grand Master, and Geoffrey de Charney,
       Preceptor of Normandy, are burnt at the stake

CHRONOLOGY OF EVENTS IN IRELAND

1168   Arrival of the first Anglo-Normans to Ireland

1169   Arrival of second group of Anglo-Normas to Ireland

1170   Strongbow arrives in Ireland

1172   King Henry II of England arrives in ireland

1175   Raymond le Gros arrives in Ireland

1175   Treaty of Windsor – John becomes Lord of Ireland

1177   Templars sign charter in Dublin

1177   Prince John of England arrives in Ireland

1210   King John of England arrives in Ireland

1220   Templars arrive in Ireland –English sources?

1220   Templars appointed to the English Treasury in Ireland

1250c Templars fall out of favour with English Crown

1254   Prince Edward granted Lordship of Ireland

1298   Edward I requests Templars to join his forces against Scots

1308   Templars arrested in Ireland. Interred at Dublin Castle

1309   Templars still at large to be imprisoned – Crown directive

1310   Inquisition at St Patrick's Cathedral

1312   Pope orders bishops of Ireland to help Hospitallers

1317   Edward Bruce crowned King of Ireland at Dundalk

1334   Hospitallers in possession of most of Templar properties

INTRODUCTION

After the success of the First Crusade in 1099 A.D. which liberated Palestine from the Egyptians, a number of knights remained on in Jerusalem to act as guardians to the pilgrims visiting the Holy Land and as protectors of the Holy Places. These two objectives were the basis of their role in the Middle East and were already being pursued by the Order of the Knights of Saint John, otherwise known as the Knights Hospitallers, which had been established c. 1071 and whose members lived in an annex of the monastery of Saint Mary of the Latins.

The group of knights who later became known as the Templars depended on King Baldwin II, the Patriarch of Jerusalem and the Canons of the Lord's Temple for their accommodation, food, and clothes. During the early years of their rough existence they were regarded more like beggars than soldiers of God because of their poor apparel and their dependency on hand-outs from the Hospitallers with whom they were friendly.

The two names associated with this early group were Hugh de Payens, from Champagne and Godfrey of Saint-Omer from Picardy in France. According to William, Archbishop of Tyre, which is situated on the Mediterranean coast of the

Holy Land, there were only nine knights for the first nine years of their existence and their life was modest and somewhat restricted due to their dependence on others.

In 1127, King Baldwin sent Hugh de Payens and some of his companions to the kings of France and England with introductory letters so that they could get some financial help and more recruits for the Holy Land. They were received by the French king and others who gave them silver and gold and also donated some lands which would generate an income.

Hugh also traveled to England and Scotland where he was well received. Ending up at the Council of Troyes in 1129 he presented his arguments for the setting up of the Order. Amongst those who were present at the Council was the abbot Bernard of Clairvaux, who drew up a set of rules based on those of the Cistercians for the new order.

Meanwhile, King Baldwin, sent William of Tyre and Roger, the bishop of Ramla, to Pope Honorius III in Rome. A Latin rule and white habit were assigned to the Templars on the orders of the pope and Stephen, the Patriarch of Jerusalem. Hugh de Payens died c. 1136 and was succeeded as Grand Master by Robert of Craon.

Around the same time, at the Council of Pisa in 1135, Pope Innocent II gave the Templars a number of donations of money and eventually laid out their privileges in his bull *Milites Templi* in 1144. They were officially now a society of 'warrior monks' whose aim was to protect pilgrims and the Holy Places while leading a monastic life.

They also became known as the *Militia Dei*, the 'Brothers of the Temple' and the 'Poor Knights of the Temple,' the 'Holy Knights of the Temple of Solomon', and the 'Knight Brothers of the Temple'. They began to accumulate wealth by the acceptance of gifts and the grants of lands. By this stage the Templars were administering the Papal State in Italy and were acting as papal treasurers and collecting money for Christian expenses in the Holy Land.

Besides the Papal State, the Templars were also receiving donations or grants of lands in France, England, Spain and Ireland for their efforts in protecting the Holy Places and also their prayers for the souls of the donor and their families. They were now becoming a strong financial institution and were in a position not only to advance loans to the kings of France, Aragon and England, but also to lords and noblemen. During the course of the second Crusade they even subsidized the expenses of the king and noblemen when they found themselves running out of funds for the subsistence of their armies on the way to the Holy Land.

Each successive pope was the overall commander of the knights and they owed allegiance solely to him. They were now an international organization which crossed national borders and did not have to worry about any obligation to ecclesiastical bishops or local clergy. Their privileges from the popes were all embracing – they did not have to pay tithes to the Church, they could receive priests into the Order, they were promised financial help from papal taxes and they were given permission to build town, churches and cemeteries in isolated places. They could not be excommunicated by any Bishop and were free from any interference from those who held power within the Church.

This freedom created a certain amount of unpopularity amongst some of clergy and the ordinary public towards the Templars. The taxes being levied by the Church c. 1175 for another Crusade brought great hardship to the people nowhere more so than in the British Isles. These amounted to a tenth of the value of all lay and clerical property. Those who did not pay up were liable to be excommunicated. All monies collected were handed over to the Templars for safe-keeping and later transferred to Rome. William of Tyre, c. 1180, who had no love for the Templars, stated that the riches of the Templars were equal to those of any king. He also accused the Templars of carrying off treasures from the Holy Land and booty captured from the Saracens.

The siege of Damietta, the fall of Damascus, the battle of Hattin in 1187 and the capture of Acre were disastrous blows to the Christian forces and they lost a substantial amount of territory as well as the city of Jerusalem. The Templars themselves lost over a thousand men in these battles and many others were taken prisoners and executed by Saladin's forces not to mention their servants, the turcopoles and mercenaries who numbered in the thousands. Those knights killed had to be replaced by new recruits from the West. These were arriving at the base in Cyprus right up to the time that the Templars were eventually arrested. During this period the animosity of the Hospitallers towards the Templars grew and led to clashes between the Orders while Saladin continued to unify the Islamic forces in the Middle East with his call for a *Jihad* against the Christians.

The Treaty of Jaffa in September 1192 between King Richard I and Saladin allowed the Christian forces to retain lands along the coast between Tyre and Jaffa but not the city of Jerusalem. The loss of Jerusalem and most of the Holy Land had a disastrous effect on the Templars. They could no longer protect the Holy Places or offer protection to those pilgrims eager to visit Jerusalem. Those in the Holy Land had nothing much to do except man the few castles which they still held along the coastline including Athlit (Pilgrim's Castle) and Safad where they placed garrisons of over 300 Templar knights.

After the time of the third Crusade in 1188 the Templars moved their main base in the Holy Land to the fortified city of Acre which came under siege the following October. With insufficient trained personnel to man the walls and lack of arms it was only a matter of time before Acre fell, but not before part of the city's defence force was evacuated by sea. The Templars had finally been driven out of the Holy Land.

By this time the Templars had been well established in England where they had many preceptories and houses. After the military success of Fitzgerald and then of Strongbow (Richard de Clare/Richard Fitz-Gilbert) in Ireland during the late 1160s and early 1170s, King Henry II of England, in 1172, decided to come to Ireland personally, fearing that Strongbow might claim the country for himself. It is generally accepted that the first Templars and Hospitallers came with either Fitzgerald or Strongbow and then a few years later more arrived with the king as part of his retinue as they were already employed as his advisors and held posts in the English Chancery.

Henry made no delay in granting lands to the Templars to finance their efforts in the Holy Land. Areas around Wexford, Waterford and Dublin were the first to be claimed by the king and transferred to the Templars. These were followed by other grants of land by the Anglo-Norman nobles in the counties of Carlow, Louth, Kilkenny, Sligo, and Limerick in addition to a number of other locations. The Templars did not waste any time and soon had a Master appointed to the Irish lands where preceptories and houses were quickly built. There is no documented account of all the houses and properties that the Templars held in Ireland. Yet, their holdings must have been substantial because the income return for Ireland as a whole was one of the highest in Western Europe.

In preparation for the third Crusade, which took place between 1189 and 1192, taxes were levied on everyone by the papal directive titled *The Ordinance of the Saladin Tithe*, 1188. This was a tax levied against one-tenth of the revenue and movables except the arms and horses of a knight (in Orders) or a cleric. The money was collected in each parish in the presence of a parish priest, the local dean, a Templar knight, a Hospitaller knight, a servant of the king and a clerk of the local bishop in order to verify that the correct amount had been collected. This was handed over to the Templars for eventual transfer to Rome. To say the least, this collection of tax did not endear the Templars and the clergy to the hearts of the ordinary people.

In addition to the raising of this tax, the clergy exhorted those who had the experience of bearing arms to volunteer for the Crusade in order to gain salvation and redemption from their sins. It is not known how many volunteered from Ireland but the records show that over 3,000 were recruited in Wales due to the exhortations of Gerald of Wales and Archbishop Baldwin. Some commentators of that period made the comment that the West was being bled dry of young men and money for a lost cause. Questions were beginning to surface about the role of the Templars who should have been organizing and preparing for the up-coming Crusade instead of increasing their wealth in Europe. Speculation as to their exact role in Christendom commenced and the secrecy surrounding the Order gave rise to rumours and accusations.

Many of the kings of Europe were envious of the Templar wealth especially Philip IV of France who had seen their treasures when he sought refuge from a mob at the Paris Temple. His aide, William de Nogaret and a priest called Esquiu de Floyran drew up a list of charges against the Templars which included heresy. These were accepted as true by Philip but not by James II of Aragon, in Spain.

Moving quickly Phillip gave the order that all Templars in his kingdom should be immediately arrested and jailed. This order was carried out on the thirteenth of October 1307. Meanwhile, Pope Clement V knew nothing of what was happening in France and admonished Philip for acting without his permission. Only he had the power to order the arrest of members of a religious Order. He then wrote to the various kings of Europe advising them to arrest, imprison and interrogate the Templars. Most of the kings obeyed the pope's orders including Edward II of England who reluctantly ordered the arrests and the confiscation of all Templar properties in January 1308. He did not, however, authorize the use of torture and none of the Templars in England confessed to the accusations brought against them. In France it was a different story. Many of the Templars confessed and died under torture while others were burned at the stake. In Ireland the king's instructions were carried out on the twenty-fifth of January 1308 and the Templars that could be located were arrested and jailed in Dublin Castle while their properties were seized. As in England, none of the Templars confessed and they were released under house arrest.

The Knights of the Hospital (Hospitallers) were allocated all the Templar properties and goods on the Continent and in England and Ireland. It took them almost 20 years to gain occupation. The Order of the Knights Templar was dissolved by Pope Clement IV on the second of May, 1312 and the religious confraternity faded into extinction.

Origins of the Knights Templar

Jerusalem was the centre of the three great faiths, Judaism, Christianity and Islam. It was where King Solomon built a large temple to house the Ark of the Covenant in 950 B.C., where Jesus Christ was buried and rose from the dead and from where Muhammad ascended into heaven. Despite the fact that Jerusalem and the Holy Land were occupied by the Muslims, Christians from the west, had made pilgrimages by land and by sea to the Holy Places for centuries.

This all changed when the Seljuk Turks conquered the Byzantine Empire and the Holy Land. Those making pilgrimages found it increasingly difficult to journey to Jerusalem and had to travel armed or with an escort of fighting men. With the many reports of the hardships endured by Christians on their way to Jerusalem including robbery, murder and slavery, Pope Urban II, in November 1095 requested that all western European kings, knights and warriors should join together and march eastwards to liberate Jerusalem and make the overland routes safe for pilgrims.

The forces of the First Crusade captured Jerusalem on the sixteenth of July 1099 and liberated the Holy Land. The Latin kingdom of Jerusalem was established with a Frankish prince called Baldwin as king. With their victory accomplished most of those who took part gradually began to return home leaving only a small force numbering in the hundreds to defend Jerusalem and the Holy Land from future attack. The crusaders were mostly Franks who were of Germanic origins then in possession of many areas of Western Europe including the Rhineland, parts of France and Sicily. Others were Flemish or English and came from important noble families in their respective countries.

The history of the Knights Templar commences in 1104 when Count Hugh de Champagne, accompanied by a number of French knights, went on pilgrimage to the Holy Land. He was the ruler of a large principality north of the city of Troyes in France. Amongst his knights was Hugh de Payens who was either a close friend or a relative. After some four years Hugh de Champagne returned to his principality in France. He once again journeyed to the Holy Land in 1114. While in Jerusalem he and Hugh de Payens, whose wife had died, met a number of knights led by a Godfrey of Saint-Omer.

After long discussions they all agreed to set up a community of knights for the defence of Jerusalem and the protection of all those pilgrims who were travelling overland to the Holy Places. In addition, they decided that they would follow the rules of a religious order and accepted those of the Canons of the Church of the Holy Sepulchre in Jerusalem.

On Christmas Day, 1119, with the approval of King Baldwin and the Patriarch of Jerusalem, they took vows of poverty, chastity and obedience. Amongst the other knights present were Archambaud of Saint-Aignan, Payes of Montdidier, Geoffrey de Bissot and a Rossal (Roland). It was decided that they should call themselves the 'Poor Fellow-Soldiers of Jesus Christ.'

As members of the new Order they continued to wear their knightly apparel. Lacking the means of existence and some

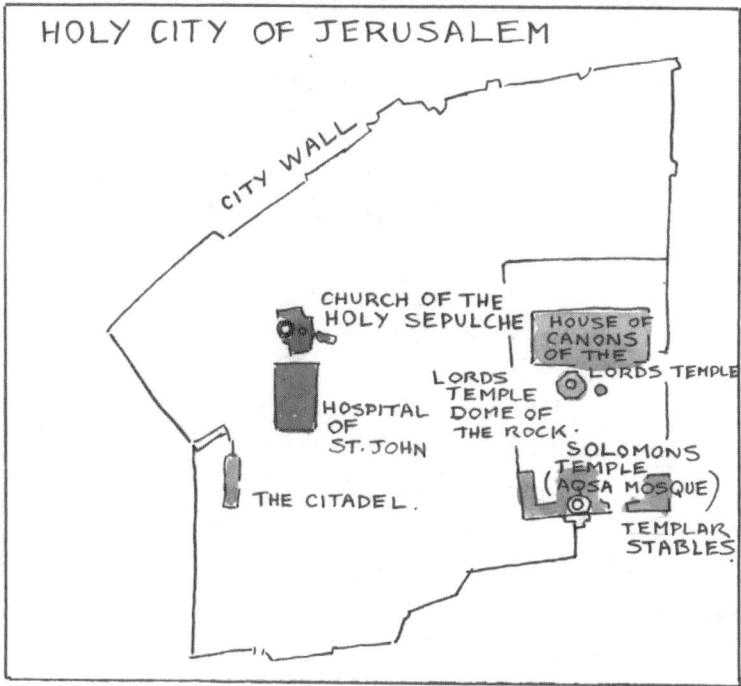

Medieval Jerusalem

place as a temporary abode, King Baldwin and the Patriarch gave them some money and endowed them with a number of benefices. They were also allocated a place to stay which was part of the building called the old *Al-Aqsa* Mosque which was situated on the southern side of the Temple Mount or the Temple of Solomon. From this humble beginning they became known as 'The Poor Fellow-Soldiers of Jesus Christ and the Temple of Solomon.' In addition, they were also called the 'The Knights of the Temple of Solomon' and 'The Knights of the Temple.'

The historian, Fulcher of Chartres, who was living and writing in Jerusalem c. 1127 makes no mention of the Templars under any of the above names. However, William, Archbishop of Tyre, writing about that time stated that the first Templars consisted of a group of noble knights from the West. He became very critical of the Order later when he stated that their successes were based on their privileged roots and exempt status in the Church which was promoted by the papacy. In fact, he was against all military Orders including the Hospitallers.

As the knights were still in only temporary accommodation, King Baldwin II (1118–1131) donated a part of his palace near the Lord's Temple, while the Canons of the Lord's Temple gave the Templars some adjoining land. They were also granted an allowance to buy food and clothing. From their early days they wore dark coloured monastic habits and became indistinguishable from other monastic Orders like the Benedictines and the Cistercians. In fact, they were often mistaken for members of the Knights of the Hospital of Saint John. All down the ages up to recent time many historians, writers and commentators have found it difficult to distinguish between the two orders.

The knights of the Hospital of Saint John had been formed sometime before 1071 as a lay community to take care of the sick, infirm and the poor pilgrims in Jerusalem and the Holy Land. In the beginning, they were a military force of knights, who later assisted the monks of Saint Mary of the Latins who had established a monastery and hospital in Jerusalem since before the first Crusade. This monastery had been founded by the merchants of Amalfi who traded with the Holy Land. The knights followed the Rule of the Augustinians and built their hospice on the site where the conception of Saint John the Baptist had been announced by an angel.

The Order was formally recognised by a papal bull in 1113 and in the following years the Hospitallers, as they became known, established a number of houses in Europe to cater for pilgrims on their way to the Holy Land. Under Raymond of

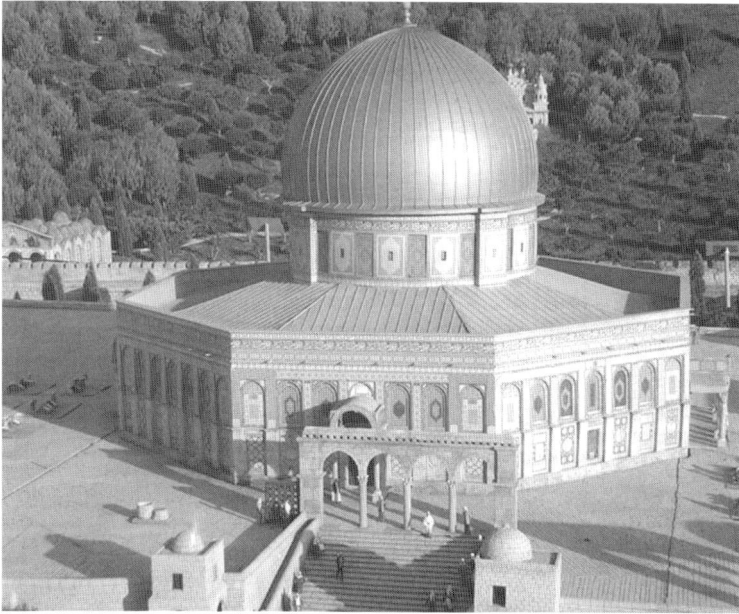

The mosque on Temple Mount today

Le Puy they returned to being a military organisation c.1120. In later years they became known as the Knights of Malta. Up to the 1120s there had been a close association between the Hospitallers and the Templars who had now become a disciplined institutionalized army.

In addition to the Order of Saint John and the Hospitallers there were other confraternities of monks in Jerusalem, namely, the Augustinian Canons of the Holy Sepulchre who looked after the Temple of the Lord (Dome on the Rock) and the Augustinian Hospitallers who also took care of ill pilgrims.

Towards the end of the thirteenth century another Order was formed. This became known as the Order of the Teutonic Knights. This Order was made up of knights who had been in the company of Frederick Barbarossa on his way to liberate the Holy Land. They were mainly from Lübeck and Bremen in Germany. They decided to remain in Jerusalem and cater for the sick, injured and infirm and founded a hospital in Jerusalem under the patronage of Saint Mary of the Germans. They later formed an Order of Knights like the Knights Hospitaller and adopted the Templar Rule. This new Order was approved by Pope Celestine III in 1196. They dressed like the Templars but had a black cross on their tunics instead of the Templar red.

Bernard of Clairvaux depicted in a thirteenth century manuscript

Some years after the founding of the Order, in order to gain recognition and to raise funds, King Baldwin and the Patriarch of Jerusalem sent a letter to Bernard seeking his approval of the Order and dispatched Hugh de Payens, Godfrey of Saint-Omer, and one Roland to the kings, nobles and religious houses of the West with introductory letters. They met with Bernard of Clairvaux at the Council of Troyes and it was he who made out a spiritual basis for their existence and gave them the Rules of the Cistercians. This was no surprise as Bernard's uncle, Andrew, had joined the Templars sometime earlier.

Afterwards they travelled around Europe, where they were welcomed by all the religious orders who gave them many donations either in money or lands. The met the king of France who gave them money and lands which could provide a steady income in the future. They met Henry, king of England in France before travelling onwards to England. They also well-received by David, king of Scotland. During the following years many noblemen from various countries joined the Templars.

Meanwhile, two other knights were sent to the pope in Rome by King Baldwin and the Patriarch. Having presented their letters of introduction they were received by Pope Innocent II, who instructed them to wear a white tunic to distinguish them from the other existing Orders. The pope exempted them from the authority of the ecclesiastical church and made them answerable to him alone. This exemption became known as the great bull *Omni Datum Optimum*.

Soon, with the support of Saint Bernard, the Order spread rapidly throughout Europe. It was immune from church tithes and members could not be excommunicated by local bishops. Later, in the time of Pope Eugenius III, a red cross was stitched on to their white mantles over their left breast as a sign of their willingness to die for Christ.

Back in the Holy Land they began to live a spiritual life when not out protecting the pilgrims. They spent their time fasting and in prayer. It is recorded that prior to this time, that the Order was so poor that they shared a horse between two as illustrated on the official seal of the order. This image did not go unnoticed and in later years built up their reputation as the poor Knights of the Temple. The fear of the kind of poverty they had endured during their early days made them careful with their resources. This later led to the belief that they were imbued with avarice and greed.

Not all the knights who joined the Order were of noble families. They were however obliged to possess a horse and all the apparel and armour of a knight warrior. Many families went into debt in order that a favourite son could become a member of the Order. These recruits were ordinary people lacking education and only possessed a knowledge of their colloquial language with very few able to write. With their long beards, soft caps on their shaven heads, long dark habits and white mantles with a red cross over the right breast they were easily recognisable to those in the Holy Land. However, they were sometimes confused with the Knights of the Hospital of Saint John (Hospitallers) who wore the same apparel except for a white cross on their mantles. Later, more confusion arose as the Order of the Teutonic Knights came on the scene wearing a black cross on their mantles to distinguish them from the others. The Templars were not religious monks as such but took the vows of poverty, chastity and obedience and were not confined to an enclosed house like other monks.

In the East, the Templars had their own particular structure which was somewhat similar to that of the Hospitallers. The Order was governed by a Master who based himself at the Templar headquarters in Jerusalem. The Master was elected for life after been chosen by an assembly of brothers living at the headquarters or elsewhere due to particular circumstances at the time. Those brothers in the West who could not attend the election, were requested to fast and pray to God for guidance. The assembly was called by the Grand Commander. He was to be distinguished from the Master of the Order and the commander (preceptor) who was responsible for all matters in the East as well as the West.

At the election there were thirteen electors – eight brothers (knights), four sergeant-brothers and a chaplain-brother – with the chaplain-brother representing Christ and the other brothers the twelve disciples. They should be chosen by a majority decision but a brother in the East should be considered before a brother from the West. The brother chosen was regarded as the spiritual head, the chief executive of the Order, who would lead the brothers into battle and who represented the Order to the outside world. The new Master was assisted by the other brothers in ruling the Order when Chapters were held to discuss any problems and to carry out the election of other members. This type of hierarchical structure was changed around the middle of the twelfth century to a *Seneschal*, Master, head military officer, a draper and a commander who was responsible for the lands of Jerusalem.

The draper was in charge of clothing and the households while the Seneschal took over the Order on the death of the Master. He later became known as the Grand Commander. There was also a banner-bearer who carried the standard of the Order into battle. The Master, for correspondence and private communications, had his own particular seal which was double sided with the circular dome of the church of the Holy Sepulchre on one side and two knights on one horse on the reverse side.

As knight brothers they were fully professional warriors. Each knight was supposed to have three horses which were large, heavy and chosen for their strength and endurance. They were armed with a sword, a coat of mail which extended over the head, a chain-mail shirt, a wide-brimmed helmet, a jacket of cloth and leather worn under the coat of mail, a triangular shield made of wood and covered in leather with the two long sides slightly curved, a Turkish mace, three knives and shoes of mail. Each had a number of servants who were on foot and armed with either a double-headed Irish axe or bows and a sword.

Going into battle the knights were accompanied by the turcopoliers (mostly Syrians on light and fast horses) and the foot mercenaries. When in battle mode and lead by the standard-bearer and the Master, the Templars were recognised as a formidable force as they rode in a close battle formation which could break through any defensive line and scatter the enemy. One can only envisage the conditions of the knights going into battle with the insufferable heat under their armour and the burning sand blowing into their faces and even penetrating their coats of mail.

By the end of the 1140s the Templars emerged as a fully-fledged military order with a hierarchical structure. This was mainly due to the efforts of Robert de Craon of Anjou (Robert of Burgundy) who had succeeded Hugh de Payens as Grand Master in 1131. He was recognised as a good administrator and organizer. Robert received the support of Count Fulk of Anjou who later became king of Jerusalem on the death of King Baldwin II. Fulk was one of the first benefactors who allotted a regular annual donation to the Order. It is said that the Templars were not immune from secular intervention and that at least seven of the Masters in the East were elected by outside influences. With the growth of the new Order of the Templars the Hospitallers became jealous and not to be outdone, they had already reverted to being a military force and began to compete with the Templars at the royal court in Jerusalem, the West and on the field of battle. At about this time the number of Templar Knights in Jerusalem was put at about 300 with the Hospitallers having approximately the same number. This combined figure was about half of the fighting force in the kingdom of Jerusalem.

Meanwhile, both Orders continued their work with the sick, infirm pilgrims who had suffered attacks and injuries as well as being robbed on their journey to the Holy Places.

As mentioned before, the Hospitallers were situated near the church of the Holy Sepulchre where they had their hospital while the Templars expanded their quarters beside the *Al-Aqsa* Mosque to include a church and additional buildings such as a hospital. It is said that the Templars during their excavations for the new buildings came across a labyrinth of tunnels running under the Dome of the Rock which was formerly the Temple of Solomon. According to historians the stone blocks used in the building of the Temple were taken from under the site where they were

The ramparts at Antioch

cut, measured and lifted to the surface, leaving a labyrinth of tunnels and passages beneath the temple. One of the myths regarding the Templars is that when they discovered these tunnels and caverns they found priceless treasures. This has never been proven and remains just a legend but it has been brought into prominence as actual fact by some writers in modern times.

After the early crusading successes and the capture of the Holy Land and Jerusalem the Frankish nobles began to divide up the conquered territory into small principalities which could be called a type of colonisation. To protect their interests

The Templar fortress of Monzun in Aragon

they began to build castles and fortification similar to those they had in the West. In the beginning, these were manned by Frankish knights and warriors. The Templars, on the other hand, began to build small fortresses and towers along the pilgrim routes to Jerusalem for the protection of the travellers through a land which in places was still hostile and infected with bandits and robbers. In time, the Frankish noblemen could no longer afford the maintenance of their castles so they handed them over to the Templars and the Hospitallers who repaired, strengthened and refortified them.

The Templars did not come into their own in castle building until King Fulk requested them to construct castles and fortifications to protect the northern and southern borders. By this time, the Templars had sufficient wealth to build additional castles and fortifications such as Sidon, Tyre, Acre, Castle Pilgrim and the Red Cistern. Most of the work was supervised by the Mason brothers who employed Syrian and Palestinian craftsmen.

These castles or fortifications could withstand a long siege due to their structure. Some of them had very strong garrisons like Saphet which had 1,500 men including 50 Knights Templar, 30 to 40 sergeant-brothers, 50 turcopoles and 300 bowmen. Their castles, which had a monastery inside the walls, were centres of religious life and administrative centres and places of refuge for the inhabitants who lived in the immediate area. They were also places from where the Templars could set out to raid Muslim caravans which passed nearby and capture people whom they could enslave or hold for ransom after taking all the goods which had some value.

As most of the Templar castles in the Middle East have vanished in time, the best existing examples are in Spain and include superb examples of the architecture of that period. Like the Franks the Anglo-Normans became renowned for their castles which dotted the landscape of France, England, Scotland and Ireland. These varied in size depending on the wealth of the individual family and whether or not its location was in the midst of warring tribes or clans. Some could be classified as fortresses, especially those which were built to strengthen the borders of the individual mini-kingdoms as was the case in Ireland where treaties were often broken and attacks followed.

The Templars followed the example of the Anglo-Normans in Ireland and built their foundations in a manner which was suitable for the particular location. Most of their castles and fortifications have now disappeared from the landscape but a few ruins are still visible. The Templar castles have been listed elsewhere in this volume.

The Templars did not spend much money on their buildings in Ireland except for their castles. What they built were modest preceptories for practical use, which differed in size and character. In England and Ireland they were mostly economic units such as rural manors. These usually contained barns to store corn, stables for the horses, and dormitories for their members, a simple church and sometimes an outer enclosing wall for protection. The size of the building complex depended on the location and the amount of land held. Some of the churches of both the Templars and the Hospitallers had a rotunda which was modelled on that of the Church of the Holy Sepulchre in Jerusalem or some other unusual features copied from the east where the best stone-masons were to be found.

THE RULE OF THE TEMPLARS

A t this point some mention has to be made regarding
the Rule of the Templar Order that evolved over some
100 years and which was so important to the lives of the
brotherhood. These Rules, translated from the French of the
monk Jean Michel, would fill a book in their own right. The
following are some of the most important excerpts which
deserve mention because they clarify some aspects of the role
of the Templars in the Holy Land and in society.

No. 3. *Prologue of Rules*
'That we, in all joy and all brotherhood, at the request of
Master Hugues de Payens, by whom the aforementioned
knighthood was found by the grace of the Holy Spirit,
assembled at Troyes from divers provinces beyond the
mountains on the feast of Saint Hilary, 1128, in the ninth
year after the founding of the aforesaid knighthood.'

No. 7. *Founders of the Order*
'And also present was Brother Hugues de Payens, Master of the
Knighthood, with some of his brothers whom he had brought
with him. These were Brother Roland, Brother Godefroy,
Brother Geoffroi Bisot, Brother Payen de Montdidier and
Brother Archambaut de Saint-Amand.'

No. 9. *Beginning of the Rules*
'You who renounce your own wills, and you others serving the sovereign king with horses and arms, for the salvation of your souls, for a fixed term, strive everywhere with pure desire to hear matins and the entire service according to canonical law and the customs of the regular masters of the Holy City of Jerusalem.'

No. 11. *The manner in which brothers should be received into the Order*
'If any secular knight, or any other man, wishes to leave the mass of perdition and abandon that secular life and choose your communal life, do not consent to receive him immediately, for thus said my lord Saint Paul: "Test the soul to see if it comes from God". Rather, if the company of the brothers is to be granted to him, let the Rule be read to him, and if he wishes to studiously obey the commandments of the Rule, and if it pleases the Master and the brothers to receive him, let him reveal his wish and desire before all the brothers assembled to chapter and let him make his request with a pure heart.'

No. 17. *On dress*
'We command that all the brothers' habits should always be of one colour, that is white or black or brown. And we grant to all knight brothers in winter and in summer if possible, white cloaks; and no one who does not belong to the aforementioned Knights of Christ is allowed to have a white cloak, so that those who have abandoned the life of darkness will recognise each other as been reconciled to their creator by the sign of the white habits; which signifies purity and complete chastity.'

No. 37. *On brothers sent overseas*
'Brothers who are sent throughout divers countries of the world should endeavour to keep the commandment of the Rule according to their ability and live without reproach with regard to meat and wine, etc. so that they may receive a good report from outsiders and not sully by deed or word the precepts of the Order, and so that they may set an example of good works and wisdom.'

No. 39. *Obedience to the Master*
'In order to carry out their holy duties and gain the glory of the Lord's joy and escape the fear of hell-fire, it is fitting that all brothers who are professed strictly obey their Master.'

No.41. *Brothers' behaviour in the outside world*
'Brothers may go in pairs, but otherwise may not go out by day or night.'

No. 51. *On animals and squires*
'Each knight-brother may have three horses and no more without the permission of the Master, because of the great poverty which exist at the present time in the house of God and of the Temple of Solomon. To each knight-brother we grant three horses and one squire, and if that squire willingly serves charity, the brother should not beat him for any sin he commits.'

No. 57. *On acquiring lands and men*
'This kind of new order we believe was born out of the Holy Scriptures and divine providence in the Holy Land of the East. That is to say that this armed company of knights may kill the enemies of the cross without sinning. You may also have lands and keep men, villains and fields and govern them justly, and take your right to them as it is specifically established.'

Nos. 65/66. *Secular knights*

'Those who serve out of pity and remain with you for a fixed term are knights of the house of God and of the Temple of Solomon. We command all secular knights who desire with a pure heart to serve Jesus Christ and the house of the Temple of Solomon for a fixed term to faithfully buy a suitable horse and arms, and everything that will be necessary for such work.'

No. 69. *Married brothers*

'If married men ask to be admitted to the fraternity, benefice and devotions of the house, we permit you to receive them on the following conditions: that after their death they leave you a part of their estate and all that they have obtained henceforth. Meanwhile, they should lead honest lives and endeavour to act well towards the brothers. But they should not wear white habits or cloaks; moreover, if the lord should die before his lady, the brothers should take part of his estate and let the lady have the rest to support her during her lifetime; for it does not seem right to us that such women should live in a house with brothers who have promised chastity to God.'

No. 70. *Regarding sisters*

'The company of women is a dangerous thing, for by it the old devil has led many from the straight path to Paradise. Henceforth, let no ladies be admitted as sisters into the house of the Temple; that is why, dear brothers, henceforth it is not fitting to follow this custom, that the flower of chastity is always maintained among you.'

(This implies that women were previously involved in the Order and not just as associates. These were probably women who took the monastic vows and were accepted into the Order.)

No. 71. *No familiarity with women*
'We believe it to be a dangerous thing for any religious to look too much upon the face of a woman. For this reason none of you may presume to kiss a woman, be it a widow, young girl, mother, sister aunt or any other; and henceforth the Knighthood of Jesus Christ should avoid at all cost the embraces of women, by which men have perished many times, so that they may remain eternally before the face of God with a pure conscience and sure life.'

No. 111. *The acquisition of items of value*
'The Commander of the Land is Treasurer of the convent, and all the belongings of the house, wherever they may be brought from here or overseas, should be given and delivered in the hands of the Commander of the Land; and he should put them in the treasury, and should not touch or remove anything until the Grand Master has seen and counted them; and when he has seen them, they should be put in writing and the Commander should keep them in the treasury and use them according to the needs of the house. And if the master or a party of worthy men of the house wishes to hear the list, he should give it to them.'

No. 116. *Spoils of war*
'All the booty, all the animals with packsaddles, all the slaves and all the livestock that the houses of the kingdom of Jerusalem gain through warfare, should be under the command of the Commander of the Land, except the saddled horses, armour and arms, which shall go to the Marshal at Arms.'

No. 119. *Money and ships*
'If the Commander needs expenses he should inform the Master, and should take what he takes with his consent.

All the ships which belong to the house at Acre are under the command of the Commander of the Land. And the commander of the shipyard at Acre and all the brothers who are there under him, are under his command, and all the things which the ships carry should be given to the Commander of the Land.'

No. 122. *The Holy Cross*
'When the True Cross is transported by horse, the Commander of Jerusalem and ten knights should guard it by day and night, and should camp as near the True Cross as they can for as long as the journey lasts, and each night two brothers should keep watch over the True Cross; and if it happens that the camp is established, everyone should lodge within the convent.'

No. 137. *Building houses*
'Nor may these Commanders (Preceptors) build new house of lime, mortar or stone without the permission of the Master. But they may rebuild and repair ruined houses.'

No. 141. *Dress*
'The surcoats (cloaks) of the sergeant brothers should be completely black, with a red cross on the front and back. And they may have either black or brown mantles.'

No. 226. *Expulsion from Order*
'He who kills or causes to be killed a Christian man or woman.'

No. 231. *Expulsion from Order*
'Whoever is found guilt of heresy or going against the law of Our Lord.'

No. 236. *Loss of habit*
'If a brother has contact with a woman, for we consider guilty a brother who enters an evil place, or a house of iniquity, with

a sinful woman, alone or in bad company; he may not keep his habit, and he may be put in irons.'

No. 254. *Kills a slave*
'If a brother kills, or wounds, or loses a slave through his own fault, he may loose his habit.'

No. 268. *Rules of the chaplain-brothers*
'The chaplain-brother should make the same promises as the other brothers; and should conduct himself like the other brothers; except for the right of the paternoster, they should say the hours. And they should wear a closed robe, and shave their beards, and may wear gloves. He should be honoured, and given the best robes of the house and should sit next to the Master at table, and should be served first.'

No. 269. *Confessions*
'The chaplain-brother should hear the confessions of the brothers; no brother should make confession to anyone else but him, because he may see the chaplain-brother without permission. For they have greater power to absolve them on behalf of the pope than an archbishop.'

No. 324. *Dress*
'No brother may wear a hood on his head. No brother may wear a coif without a cloth cap. Each brother is obliged to honour his habit and should not hang his mantle round his bed on hooks.'

No. 329. *Money*
'Each brother of the Temple, both the Master and others, should assiduously take care that he does not keep money for himself, neither gold or silver, for a person of religion should not have anything of his own.'

No. 337. *Knightly class*
'No brother, unless he is the son of a knight or descended from the son of a knight, should wear a white mantle.'

No. 410. *Application of justice*
'No brother of the Temple may be convicted by any secular man or by a man of another Order, nor by two or more, except by the brothers of the Temple.'

418. *Penances or expulsion*
'If a brother is tainted with the filthy, stinking sin of sodomy he should be expelled from the house for ever.'

422. *Penances or expulsion*
'If a brother is found to be a heretic, that is if he does not believe in the articles of faith in which the Church of Rome believes and commands him to believe.'

443. *Sickness or leprosy*
'When it befalls any brother that by the will of Our Lord he contracts leprosy and the thing is prove, the worthy men of the house should admonish him and ask him to request permission to leave the house and go to Saint Lazarus, and take the habit of a brother of Saint Lazarus.' (The Order of Saint Lazarus was founded in the Holy Land c.1130. It followed the Rule of Saint Augustine and received many privileges and donations. It was not confirmed by the papacy until 1255. The knights of this Order wore a green cross on their mantles).

511. *Penance*
'And let it be known that the brother who holds chapter should give corporal punishment to all the brothers who are on penance.'

Command Structure of the Templars in the East

This structure was almost the same as a military organisation in the West except for some changes to suit the Order. Elected by the eastern Chapter and subject to its views the Master had overall control of operations. It was up to him to declare war or arrange a truce or peace. He could also claim land or take over a castle or fortification when requested. Also, he had the power to appoint commanders and officers to his forces.

Next to him in authority was the Seneschal, who looked after the administration of the lands, house, food and pack train when the knights were on the move. It was also his duty to protect the Templar battle standard. Next came the Marshal whose duties included the responsibility of all military equipment and the allocation of horses to the members. After him in seniority was the Commander of the City of Jerusalem who was responsible for protection pilgrims on their way to the Holy City. He had ten knights under his command as well as turcopoles and servants. The commander also acted as treasurer to the Order. The commander of the houses and the commander of the knights came next in order. The duties of the commander of the knights were mostly confined to giving orders on the battlefield. Below these came the knight-brothers who were of the knightly class in the West. These were distinguishable by their white robes and red cross. Finally, came the sergeant-brothers who wore black or brown and were commanded by a turcoplier, who was a trained Syrian horseman, when under arms. The Templars were a military disciplined body of warrior monks who were the envy of all Western kings and princes when they observed them in battle riding against the enemy lines in a phalanx formation.

THE TEMPLARS IN THE WEST

In the West, all the properties of the Order were divided into provinces with each having its own hierarchy of officials which was slightly different to that of the East. The division followed the predominant language of each territory. One house of each province was used as a centre of administration and where all records were kept. In England, the main house or Temple was situated in London, in northern France it was at Paris while in Spain it was at Miravet. A yearly provincial chapter was held at these locations where problems were discussed, the collection of monies and other matters concerning the province which was ruled by a Master.

It seems that Ireland, being governed from the London Temple, did not have a house of administration in its own right. Under these provincial centres there were houses called preceptories where the preceptor or commander ruled like the lord of the manor. There were a number of preceptories in Ireland and these will be discussed later.

The preceptor looked after the running of the estate, his companions, tenants, hired help, seeing that the laws were enforced and that all monies or rents due were paid on time. He was responsible for sending the proceeds of the estate less ten per cent and all rents etc. to the provincial headquarters. The deduction of ten per cent was to finance the estate for the following year. He was also obliged to keep a record of all donations or monies received which were forwarded or collected. As religious houses, some preceptories employed women as dairymaids and laundresses but it is unknown whether these stayed at the preceptory. The conditions of each preceptory depended on its particular location and importance. In Ireland and parts of France they were enclosed by a high outer wall as protection. The brothers had to defend themselves and those seeking refuge within the walls. The preceptories were devoid of luxuries and mostly resembled the dwellings of poor farmers.

The main houses or temples were the principal bases for the members of the Order in the various provinces of Western Europe. Those who lived within were of a higher status than those dwelling in the preceptories. These were professed Templars, associates or pensioners of the Order. In addition to the Master, those that were fully professed were usually the chaplains, knight-brothers, sergeant or serving brothers and sisters.

The non-military sergeants or serving brothers did the manual work and included in their numbers were smiths and stone masons. When not engaged in work they were to fast and pray like other monks. The priest (chaplain) brothers of the Order were not subject to the local bishops and did not have to be of knightly birth to become chaplains. The role of the sisters and the associated members was to pray and engage in matters spiritual.

In the Order, the knight-brothers were the most important even though they were vastly outnumbered by sergeant-brothers. The knight-brothers were mostly knights i.e. trained professional soldiers who fought on horseback using the lance and the sword. Some commentators of that time stated that the knight-brothers in the East were dirty and unkempt. This would not be unusual due to the conditions under which they had to fight. During the later half of the twelfth century the role of the knight became very important in warfare in the countries and minor principalities of Western Europe. Their role in various armies, with their cavalry charge, became a part of warfare which was most feared. With the continuous fighting between the various principalities a shortage of recruits to the Order began to be experienced. This was the reason why the Master in the East introduced paid mercenaries into the Templar force.

At about the same time auxiliaries were allowed to become full members. Up to this time and from the beginning of the Order, its squires and servants were permitted to full membership. These men became sergeant-brothers or serving brothers who acted as fighting warriors or unarmed servants to the knights of the Order. In fact, most of the Templars were sergeant-brothers and those who had experience of fighting were sent to the East. These brothers were not allowed the white mantle which was reserved for the knights but continued wearing the black habit and thus often became confused with the Hospitallers in the Holy Land.

The Templars followed the monastic traditions like other contemporary Orders based around the traditional day of prayers ('hours') and work. Those who were unable to attend were obliged to recite thirteen *Pater Nostra* (Our Father) for matins, seven for each hour and nine for vespers during their absence. The day for the Templars commenced with the reading or reciting of 'the Days' beginning with Matins which was followed by private meditation. The members were to be obedient and silent where possible. Swearing was forbidden as well as drunkenness and gambling. When engaged in the rules and daily customs it would be difficult to recognise them as knights. For the most part they usually adhered strictly to the rules. In fact, they were no different from the other Orders when confined to their monasteries. However, they were not totally enclosed but had to go out to work or fight. Most of the members were not educated and could not read or write Latin. In these circumstances, the chaplain read the 'hours' for all the confraternity when the need arose. Some of the major religious works were translated into Anglo-Norman French which gave some of the members the opportunity of reading the Old and New Testament themselves.

The Blessed Virgin (Our Lady Saint Mary) was always included in their prayers because she was the patron of the Templars as she was to the Cistercians and other Orders. In addition, The Knights Templar venerated the head of Saint Euphemia, a martyr of the fourth century when they were in Jerusalem. The head was stored in a silver reliquary and with other relics was moved from location to location when there was any danger. This relic, which at times was mistaken for the head of John the Baptist; the head of a Muslim idol or the head of Jesus, was to become the basis of many accusations against the Order during their inquisition and later the basis of many legends.

Like the other Orders such as the Cistercians, Augustinians and Hospitallers, women were excluded from joining the Templars. Yet, in the West they were accepted in special circumstances. Those that were admitted brought money, influence, gifts, donations and the support of their families. One of the rare exceptions was the Templar nunnery at Mühlen in Germany. Records show that in other locations there were also a number of women living in the preceptories with the Templars. These were segregated and had their own living quarters, church and choir. Some women of high standing followed their husbands into the Order where they embraced the rules of the Order with other women. Some of these who were not professed into the Order became associate-Members with the possibility that they might join at a later stage. Those that did enter the Order were accepted after a special period of training which was a type of novitiate. The ceremony of profession was supposed to be private but all the family and friends were allowed to attend.

Catalonia in Spain was the main location where women were allowed to join the Order. It was also the place where there were a number of nunneries and slave women were engaged in work at the preceptories. There is almost a complete lack of information regarding women joining the Templars in Ireland and England. From the records available it is very unlikely that any woman was accepted into the Order in Ireland. In contrast, there is a mention of at least two noble women joining the Order as associate-members in England. However, in Spain there were the Sisters of the Order of the Temple who had their own preceptories and the head sister was referred to as the preceptrix (female preceptor) and had the same powers as her male counterparts. In Ireland, there are vague references to female serfs, bondswomen, dairymaids and laundresses in a few of the preceptories.

Meanwhile in England there were women who joined the Order and took the vows of chastity, poverty and obedience and lived in separate quarters of the houses but there is no evidence of where they exactly lived. These were mostly made up of widows of advanced age who had donated their possessions to the Order on entering, either for the salvation of their souls or to pray for the struggle in the Holy Land. Any rich widow of advanced age who wanted to spend her final days was accepted as a member of the Templar Order.

Even though the Rule forbade the Templars from having any contact with women under the pain of expulsion from the Order, it seems there were some exceptions and women were admitted to the preceptories with their husband acting as guarantees of good conduct. These women gave generous gifts of rents and lands to the Templars. Some modern day historians like Helen Nicholson think that some women were allowed to become members of the Order and allowed to live within the preceptory walls. This suggestion is based on certain accounts of the Templars in Germany and Spain.

There is no clear evidence that women were allowed to join the Order in Ireland except those who were elderly or wards of the Church. There was the possibility that women who were considered wards of the church had to be accommodated and looked after if required, especially those who had made generous donations to the Order. There are no accounts of Templars in Ireland involved with women until the subject was mentioned during the inquisition in England and France. In the Primitive Rule of the Templars No. 70 women are mentioned – 'henceforth, let not ladies be admitted as sisters into the house of the Templars.' This might mean that women were previously admitted to the Order.

The historian Foley stated that there were examples of women who took the normal monastic vows being accepted into the Templar Order. This statement seems to be justified as the Templars had a nunnery at Mühlen in Germany whose members were referred to as Sisters of the Order of the Temple. It is recorded that these nuns refused to join the Order of Hospitaller nuns after the dissolution of the Templars. There were also occasions when the German barons gave bondswomen to the Templars as a gift.

In Spain, the situation was somewhat different to the rest of Europe, where women could inherit land or the proceeds thereof. The Order could not refuse substantial donations and bent the Rules to accommodate the donors. Women who wished to take up a religious life were allowed to join the Order as associate-members with their own separate accommodation at preceptories. There were various types of associate women members who wore different religious habits. Individual nunneries were established in parts of Catalonia. The most important of these was at Rourell which had its own preceptrix who had the same powers as her male counterpart in a preceptory. It is even recorded that certain nobles, possible family relations, gave donations of land in 1198 to women who had taken up the religious life with the Templars. Also in Spain, married couples were allowed to become associate members of the Order.

*　*　*

By the 1280s the Templars had many knights and soldiers in the East. In addition they had numerous houses in the various kingdoms. They also built many castles along the pilgrim routes and at places of importance. To maintain all of these, those brothers in the West sought patronage from the various kings, lords, princes and nobility.

On the north-south route they built castles or fortifications stretching from Celecia (southern Turkey) to Jerusalem in the south and included La Roche de Roussel, Antioch, Tortosa, Beirut, Sidon, Tyre, Acre, Castle Pilgrim and Jaffa. For the protection of those pilgrims landing at Haifa or Acre and on their way to Jerusalem there were the castles of Haifa, Destroit, Safad, Saffran, Caco, La Feve, Nablus, Castle Arnald, Quarantene and the Red Cistern were among a total of some 40 castles which were not just plain fortifications but strong and magnificent edifices which could withstand any attack or siege. From these castles the Templars carried out raids against the Muslim caravans and captured people and goods which could be ransomed. The proceeds were used to sustain their castles and efforts in the Holy Land. When a caravan of pilgrims arrived at the northern castles they were escorted south to Jerusalem.

On one occasion, when the pilgrims, escorted by the Templars, were attacked by a band of Muslim renegades, they were defeated by the Templars under the leadership of Gilbert de Lacy who we find in Ireland some years later. In addition, they also escorted kings, princes and people of importance visiting the Holy Land and were advisors to the king of Jerusalem and other Latin principalities.

When Philip of Alsace visited the Holy Land in 1177 a man called Odo of Saint Armand was the Master of the Templars. He had, at that time, a force of some 84 knights under his command as well as mercenaries while he escorted Philip through the Holy Land. The number of Templar knights who were based in the Holy Land at the height of their activities is hard to ascertain. Some sources relate that the Templars and the Hospitallers together could muster about 300 fighting knights each. This force was augmented by the large number of mercenaries who were in the pay of the Templars when required.

The Templars accompanied many of the expeditions to the Holy Land. Some were successful but many failed. In the latter, the Templars were usually blamed for giving wrong advice or not agreeing with those in charge as happened after the failure of the Crusade of King Louis VII of France. Even though the Templars suffered serious losses and a number of defeats they were praised by Bernard of Clairvaux and successive popes for their courage.

* * *

The Templar built quite a few castles in Western Europe at the request of various kings and princes. These were mostly built in territories where there was a lack of civil power and the possibility of attack. They also built castles on the disputed borders of certain principalities where the princes were prone to engage in fighting. In Ireland, which was in a state of continuous conflict, they built a number of castles in strategic locations which were close to the newly acquired lands of the Anglo-Normans.

As for their preceptories and houses, these were very modest and did not require much expenditure or maintenance. With all the expenses involved in assisting the crusades money ran short and the Templars were obliged to sell some of the booty captured from the Muslims in the East. At the height of their success the Templars are said to have had about 9,000 establishments in the West while the number attributed to the Hospitallers was in excess of this figure.

Having established their religious houses in Europe, the Templars were called to royal councils and became involved in the affairs of the various rulers. Earlier, from the time of the decline of the Roman Empire, monks and other religious men, who were educated, were called to the royal courts to act as trustworthy advisors and officials and became the main protagonists in secular administration. The word 'cleric' became 'clerk' for some of these advisors.

At that time, as a result of the renaissance in culture, people began to learn to read and write both in their own language and in Latin. These people became known as the *literati* (literate) and from the thirteenth century onwards began to occupy high places in government, much to the disgust of the old nobility, who saw them as taking over their own rightful place in the administration of the courts. The military Orders were well-appreciated for their role in the employment of nobles, monarchs and the papacy and were well-compensated for their assistance. This new occupation for the Templars was to cost them dearly in later years.

Templar fortress of Soure, Portugal

The role of the Order in Europe, such as in the British Isles, France, Italy, and Spain was also of military assistance. In Rome, the pope's chamberlain, was either a Templar, Hospitaller or a Cistercian. The main services that the different Orders offered the different rulers were those of personal messengers, treasurers and judge-delegates, whilst the Templars offered financial guidance and assistance. They were entrusted to handle large sums of money and became financial couriers and almoners. This was nothing new as they regularly carried large sums from the West to the Middle East. In the beginning they were not bankers in the modern sense but accepted money, jewellery, precious stones, and other items of value for safe-keeping at the London and Paris Temples. These personal deposits remained untouched in strongboxes until required by the owner. During the period 1148 to 1230 the Templars loaned money to various kings including those of France, Aragon and England. In France, Louis IX had Brother Amaury de la Roche as his trusted advisor while in England Henry II had Brother Aimery de Saint Maur in a similar position.

From this time onwards a section of the Templars lost sight of the main objectives of the Order, i.e. the protection of pilgrims in the East and the fight against the Muslims. In fact, the Templars became fragmented into a number of groups – those fighting in the East, those at the various courts of Europe, those managing and running the estates and finally, the bankers. The Templars were not the only Order to get involved in the materialistic culture of the thirteenth century. The Cistercians and the Franciscans also took advantage of the chance of making money. If these Orders had been brought to trial, like the Templars, their activities could have been shown in a similar light.

Templar Wealth and Shipping

In the course of time the Templars became known for their pride and avarice. It is even related that King Richard, the Lionheart, on his death bed said that the Cistercians were known for their greed, the Dominicans and Franciscans for their lives of luxury and the Templars for their pride. In fact, the Templars were regarded as a miserly lot who were slow to give alms to the poor compared to the other Orders. Pope Innocent III said that the Templars were guilty of the sins of pride and avarice. He even reprimanded them for exploiting the privilege of saying Mass in churches that he had placed under interdict in order to benefit from the tithes.

They were also chastised for allowing people, even thieves, murderers and sometimes those who were excommunicated, to join a Templar confraternity as long as they were willing 'to pay two or three pence'. The pope went further, saying that 'they exhaled their greed for money'. Walter Map, Archdeacon of Oxford, writing in the early 1170s, criticised the Templars for their avarice and extravagance and for abandoning the vows of poverty and charity of their founder, Hugh de Payens. In fact, most of the writers of that time criticised the Templars for their avarice including William, Archbishop of Tyre.

Another accusation levied against the Templars was over their demand for secrecy within their own ranks and the ban of making public the proceedings of their Chapters and the reception of new members, which gave rise to suspicion regarding the overall operation of the Order. There were also doubts about their exact role in the protection of the Holy Places and of pilgrims journeying through the hostile lands, where they were more eager to attack Muslim caravans for slaves and booty.

One of the major accusations against the Templars was that despite all the privileges granted by various popes, only a small minority of their numbers were actually sent to the Holy Land. Most of their members were assigned to the position of looking after their manors and properties throughout Europe which exceeded 9,000. In addition, many Templars were occupied as almoners, advisors, treasurers etc. to the royal courts of Europe, where they were held in high esteem for their advice and trustworthiness.

From their role in charge of the treasuries of the various kings they soon became bankers, offering various financial services including lending money. In fact, the Paris Temple became one of the major financial centres of Europe where over 4,000 Templars were employed. No figures are available for the numbers at the London Temple who carried out the same financial services. Even though they were forbidden under Canon Law to charge interest on loans they still managed to charge rates which were lower than other money lenders including the Jews. From their involvement with money it is no wonder that they were accused of avarice. As a matter of interest, the Templars did not identify each client's account or deposit by name but by a number. This seems to be first instance of numbered private accounts, a practice which Swiss banks followed centuries later.

It should be noted here that all the religious Orders at the time were accustomed to lend money. With the expansion of economic activity from 1285 onwards it is no wonder that the financial position of the Templars gave rise to much envy and resentment amongst the secular clergy, other Orders and the kings, princes and barons throughout Europe. Yet, nobody realised or took into account the enormous expense which was continuously incurred by the Templars in the Holy Land where they had to clothe, accommodate, feed and arm themselves as well as many thousands of trained mercenaries. They also had to cover the costs involved in the repair, upkeep and defence of the almost 50 castles in the East which were under their control. Their properties in the East were so extensive that Pope Gregory VIII reprimanded them for acquiring Christian lands instead of regaining the former Christian lands now being held by the Muslims.

Amongst their many important clients were the kings of Aragon and France who were continuously borrowing money and at times the Templars were placed in a difficult situation – whether to comply with the requests of the kings or send badly needed funds to the their brothers in the East. In return for these loans the Templars accepted as security the annual income from certain lands or benefices.

From the middle of the thirteenth century donations to the Templars fell into decline so that they had to generate more income from their own properties including rents and tithes which amounted to 10 per cent of all produce from their tenants. Their tenants in Ireland were mostly Irish who had come with the donated properties but some were English and Welsh settlers who had been invited over by the Templars. Being short of tenants they granted tracts of land for cultivation to individual land owners.

* * *

Shipping

Before the fall of Acre and the change of the Templar base to Cyprus the Order had a number of ships of different types, such as galleys designed for cargo, passengers and goods, horses and soldiers and those dedicated to war. Little is known about the design of the ships in the Mediterranean during the twelfth and thirteenth century but details have been preserved of the ships trading out of Genoa and Venice in the mosaics at Saint Marco in Venice.

These ships were usually about 86 feet from stem to stern, had a beam of 21 or 22 feet and depth from railing to keel of about 21 feet. They had two complete decks and two cabins at the stern. They were two- or three-masted with double rudders and some had a forecastle. Their sails were of the lateen type i.e. three-cornered, secured to a long yard. The warships were of a different design and an advanced type of the earlier Roman biremes and triremes with two or three banks of oars on each side and a ram built high on the prow. The ships that traded on the western seaboard of Europe were mostly a type of galley but sailed by either lateen or square sails. They usually had two or three masts and could transport 50 to 100 tons.

From the middle of the twelfth century the Templars were using sea transport from France and Italy to the Holy Land to transport pilgrims, supplies, equipment and money. On the return journey, pilgrims, sick and injured and goods were accommodated. During the outward voyage from Marseilles, the ships which were small and could not carry much drinking water and food, required making land at Sicily, Cyprus, Crete or Rhodes before arriving at either Beirut, Jaffa, Tyre or Acre. Many of the ships departed early in spring, when weather conditions were good, so that the pilgrims would arrive at

Jerusalem for Holy Week celebrations. About this time, the master of the fortress of Acre became the commander of Templar fleet.

After the second Crusade, to avoid hostile Asia Minor, more and more pilgrims required passage by sea. To accommodate these, the Templars and the Hospitallers either bought or hired suitable ships for the voyage. Horses were transported in sailing galleys which had appropriate holds. The horses, at the destination, were lifted out by block and tackle either onto landing barges or the quayside depending on the port. Another type of ship powered by sail and oars was introduced in the trade. This was called the *buss* and had an opening and a ramp at the stern. This type of ship, which could carry up to 40 horses, was able to manoeuvre with stern to the beach so that the horses could disembark.

With the overland journey through Asia Minor becoming more dangerous each year, the fleets of the Templar and the Hospitallers became larger. In 1191, with the addition of many hired ships King Richard (the Lionheart) and his crusaders were transported to the east by sea. To accomplish this feat one can only guess at the number of ships used. On the way the island of Cyprus was captured by King Richard's

The siege of Damietta

forces but already running out of money Richard sold the island to the Templars for 25,000 marks. They later resold the island to Guy de Lusingnan, the then king of Jerusalem, with a slight profit.

From the time of the siege of Damietta (Egypt) in 1218, where both the Templar and Hospitaller ships took part, the number of ships that both Orders possessed varies according to sources. Some relate that the Templars had only four ships while the Hospitallers had a greater number. Perhaps this number only applied to their warships which were powered by Muslim slave oarsmen.

In 1220 the Templars had to hire a Genoan ship to transport pilgrim supplies and money to the East. Both Orders ran into difficulties with the use of Marseilles as their base from c.1233. The local ship owners objected to the free use of the port by both Orders when they themselves had to pay cargo dues to the local authorities. As a result the Templars were restricted to two ships *per annum*, one in the Spring and the other in early Autumn. Following this embargo the Templars began to use the ports of Collioure and Monaco. In 1287 the Templar ships attempted to attack Tripoli but had to give up due to a storm. At about the same time both the Templars and the Hospitaller warships assisted King James II of Aragon in his attack on Moorish Minorca.

After the fall of Acre in 1291 the Hospitallers, who by now had a substantial fleet of warships, began to engage, attack and sink any Muslim ship they encountered in the Eastern Mediterranean. Crews were taken as slaves and they removed whatever booty they could find. They were soon joined by the Templar warships which were all captained by Templar brothers and they both engaged in a type of piracy. Mentioned in the records is an ex-Genoan ship under the command of a Roger de Flor who was a sergeant-brother of

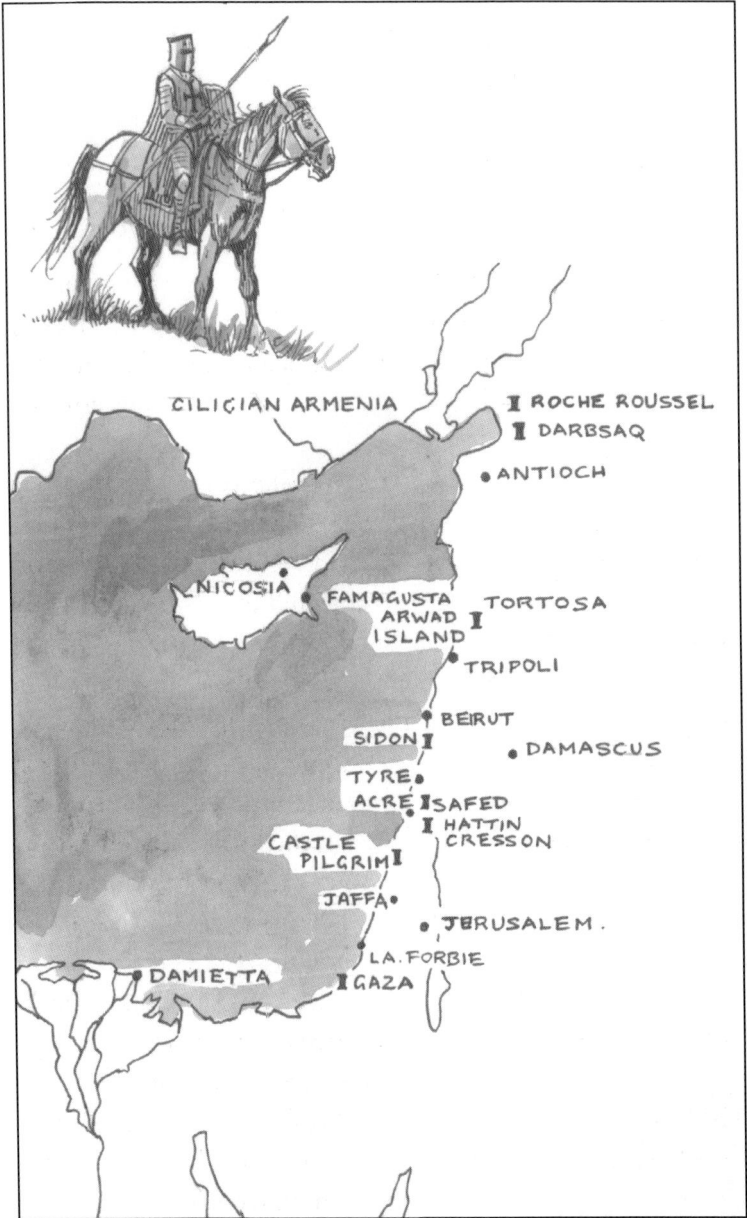

The Eastern Mediterranean at the time of the crusades

the Order. He became notorious as a pirate especially in the Aegean Sea. The pope at that time requested the Templars to prepare a large fleet to assist the Armenians, defend Cyprus and to harass the Saracen shipping. The result was that all Muslim trade had to be transported overland between Egypt and Constantinople. In the records there are details of a charter of a Genoan ship called the *Sanctus Johannes,* which must have been large as it had a crew of 55 sailors as well as servants aboard. The cost of a three-and-a-half month charter was 3,000 Saracen Besants with 2,000 paid in advance.

La Rochelle, on the Atlantic coast of France was known as the Templar fleet base from the end of the twelfth century. From here their ships traded along the coat of Western Europe from Lisbon in the south to Denmark, England and Ireland in the north. They traded in Gascon wine to England and Ireland landing at Bristol, Dover and Portsmouth in England and in Waterford, Dingle, and the Shannon in Ireland. Two of the ships involved in this trade were called the *La Bussard* and the *Le Templere.*

It is recorded in the English Patent Rolls that a Templar brother called Thomas built a 'great ship' in Portsmouth for King Henry III and in 1227 organised a muster of a fleet of over 200 ships at that port for the king. Much has been written about the 'ghost fleet' of the Templars which was based on nothing but legend. In this regard, the Templars are supposed to have visited Nova Scotia and New England in the North America, as well as the Caribbean, centuries before Christopher Columbus. Refer to the last chapter for further details.

The Battle of Hattin

On the first of July 1187, Saladin's forces crossed the river Jordan at Sennabra on the south-western side of Lake Tiberias. He had mustered a large force of some 30,000 foot soldiers and 12,500 horsemen who had come to join him from Aleppo, Damascus, Mosul and as far away as Egypt. This was the largest force that he had ever commanded. Camp was set up near a good water source at Al-Ashtara. While there, half his force captured the town of Sennabra while the remainder moved to the nearby hills.

When Guy of Lusignan, king of Jerusalem, was informed of the movements of Saladin's army he immediately gave orders that all the Christian forces should gather at Acre. Within weeks some 20,000 soldiers and 12,000 fighting horsemen had gathered including the Knights Templar and the Hospitallers.

King Guy felt that they should wait and see what Saladin would do. He could not keep together such a large army for long in the burning heat of summer. However, the fool-hardy Reginald of Chatillon, Prince of Antioch and Gerard de Rideford, the Templar Master, proposed an immediate attack. Ramond of Tripoli was completely against the move but capitulated. Orders were given for the army to march towards Tiberias and on the evening of the third of July the Christian forces camped near Sephoria tired, exhausted from the burning heat and parched from lack of water. Many had fallen by the wayside unable to continue any further. These were beheaded and stripped of their armour and arms by the Muslims who were keeping a close watch for stragglers in the moving army.

That night, news arrived at the camp that Ramond's wife had sought refuge in the citadel of Tiberias. Ramond, rather than going to rescue his wife, announced that the Christian forces should stay where they were. However, during the night, Gerard de Ridefort convinced the king of Jerusalem that the army should march and confront the Muslims.

At dawn the following morning orders were given that the force should prepare to march. The burning sun was already beating down on the parched earth as the army struggled towards Tiberias while enduring a continuous rain of arrows from the Muslim archers, which took a heavy toll on the foot soldiers. As the heat and thirst intensified many were unable to continue and groups broke off from the marching column as they observed knights falling off their horses.

Exhausted and dying of thirst the Christian forces finally made camp for the night on a high plain near Lubiya where they were surrounded by the Muslim army. Soon it was discovered that the deep water well was dry and when the wagon train did not arrive no food could be cooked. Everyone had to try and sleep with a parched throat and an empty stomach. They got little rest as the Muslims set fire to the scrubland upwind sending smoke and sparks towards the camp. As fires broke out the soldiers had to contend with a continuous hail of arrows from Saladin's archers.

By dawn the camp was in complete disarray and seizing the opportunity Saladin ordered an immediate attack from all sides. The Christian forces drove back the Muslim force on many occasions but suffered heavy losses with each assault. Count Raymond, with his horsemen engaged the enemy and finally managed to break through towards the Sea of Galilee where they could find water. Sometime later, unable to return to the main army, they had no option but to head for the safety of Tripoli.

Meanwhile, most of the infantry fled the battle lines and headed towards the two nearby hills. These were soon joined by the knights whose horses had fallen. Surrounded on all sides, what remained of

Guy De Lusignan, King of Jerusalem

the Christian force formed a circle around the king and the Bishop of Acre who held the relic of the Holy Cross.

Eventually, exhausted and unable to continue fighting those surviving were overwhelmed and taken prisoner. King Guy, Reginald of Chatillon, Gerard of Ridefort, and the knight Humphrey of Toron were taken to Saladin's tent where Saladin offered King Guy some cold water. Reginald grabbed the goblet but before he could drink, Saladin knocked it out of his hands, giving him the option of converting to Islam or dying, Reginald laughed in his face. Infuriated, Saladin drew his scimitar and cut off his head.

Later, King Guy and the barons were escorted to Damascus while the surviving Templars and Hospitallers were held captive and given the opportunity of denying their faith or facing death. At dawn the following morning approximately 250 knights had their heads cut off by the Sufis.

Between 1164 and 1250 the Templars suffered substantial losses defending the Holy Land. But it was at the Battle of Hattin in July 1187 that they suffered the greatest number of casualties. This battle was the death knell for the Christian military forces in the Middle East. Despite the bravery of

The battle of Hattin

the Templars and the Hospitallers the Christian forces were annihilated. The Templars lost over 250, not to mention their turcopoles and footsoldiers. The Muslims had by this time learned to negate the charge of the Templars by slashing the haunches of their horses bringing down both horse and knight. Those that survived the debacle retreated to Jerusalem knowing that the city would fall within weeks. The remaining Templars knew that they first had to remove their treasures, relics and everything of value to the fortress of Acre.

On a point of note, six of the Grand Masters died in battle or in captivity. As quoted in the trials, some 20,000 Templars died in the Middle East. Most of those that were taken prisoners chose to die rather than deny their faith.

After Hattin most of the Christian fortresses and castles including Acre, Tyre, Nablus, Tiberias, Sidon, Beirut, Ascalon, and Gaza surrendered to Saladin's forces within a short period of time. Only Tyre and Jerusalem remained in Christian hands.

With the whole land under his power Saladin marched on Jerusalem. Those inside the city, when given an ultimatum to surrender or face an assault on the walls, replied to Saladin that they would raze the Dome on the Rock and set fire to the city. Eventually, a truce was negotiated whereby the inhabitants would be spared regardless of religion and those who wished to leave would be given safe exit to the coast. Finally, on the second of October, 1187, Saladin entered the city in triumph. The Temple of the Holy Sepulchre was evacuated and the few remaining Templars were driven from the *Al-Aqsa* mosque.

Now, with Jerusalem under his control, Saladin marched to the fortress of Kerak where he left part of his army to carry out a siege. Montreal, Safed, Gaston and Belvoir fell to Saladin's forces shortly afterwards. The Templars, however, held on to the castles of Krak des Chevaliers, Chastel Blanc and Tortosa while the fortresses of Antioch, Tripoli and Tyre remained in Christian hands.

A medieval image of the siege of Antioch

EVENTS LEADING UP TO THE FALL OF ACRE

The news of the defeat of the Christian forces at Hattin was received with general disbelief in the West. The Templar losses had to be replaced and a major recruitment drive commenced while the preceptors of all holdings were requested to generate a larger return so as to cover the expenses of buying horses, equipment and supplies.

Within two years another Crusade was called by Pope Gregory VIII to liberate the Holy Land from the Mamaluk forces. This was to be lead by King Richard I of England and those who agreed to take part were King Philip Augustus of France; Theolbald, Count of Blois; Ralph, Count of Clermont; Henry, Count of Champagne; and many more French counts, German barons and bishops. In April of 1189, King Frederick of Germany, otherwise known as Barbarossa, also decided to take part. Already an old man who had taken part in the Second

Frederick Barbarossa in a thirteenth century chronicle

Saladin on his throne, from a twelfth century Arabic codex

Crusade he sent envoys to Saladin requesting the return of the Holy Land to the Christians. Saladin's reply was that he would release all Christian prisoners and give back the Christian churches to their monks. This was unacceptable to King Frederick so he ordered his forces to be prepared to march to the Holy Land. With the arrival of fine weather, Frederick set out on the long journey with his large army in May of that year. Unfortunately, after defeating the Seljuk Turks, Frederick fell off his horse while crossing the Calycadnus River in Armenia. Weighed down by his armour he drowned before help arrived. With the death of their king and after experiencing thirst, hunger and the inhospitable lands through which they had to travel many of his barons decided to return home with their forces. The old king's son, also called Frederick, decided to proceed to Antioch with what remained of the army.

King Guy of Jerusalem was released by Saladin in 1189 and immediately tried to take command over the Christian forces at Tyre. He encountered the opposition of Conrad Monferrat and headed to Acre. In a short space of time he had gathered a fair sized army and began to besiege the Muslim held city and fortress. Together with the forces of Philip Augustus, who had just arrived with his forces, he was unable to dislodge the Muslims from the city.

Before he left England, King Richard, in order to finance the venture, increased taxes on everything, so much so that the country was almost bankrupt. He set out in July 1190 and marched south through France. When he arrived at Marseilles the English fleet awaited him. First, arriving at Cyprus accompanied by some Templars, he captured the island in 1191 and overthrew the Emperor Comnemus. The Templars purchased the island from King Richard for 25,000 marks as he was running out of money and then resold it to a Guy de Lusingnan sometime later. When this became known in the West rumours of the Templars greed and avarice began to spread both in England and France.

King Richard arrived at the siege of Acre by sea on the eighth of June and the construction of siege towers and catapults began. On the twelfth of July the walls were breached and the city was taken. King Richard, Philip and Duke Leopold V, who had taken over what was left of Barbarossa's army, began arguing over the spoils of the captured city.

King Richard and Philip of France then commenced quarreling over who was the rightful king of Jerusalem.

Richard I of England (the Lion Heart) from a twelfth century codex

Richard declared that King Guy was the rightful king but Philip wanted Leopold on the throne. It was finally agreed that Guy would retain the title until his death and then Leopold would succeed him. Richard then decided to leave Acre and marched toward Jaffa and recaptured the city. Saladin arrived with his force and tried to tempt Richard to come out of the walled city. When he finally did emerge he had the Hospitallers on his right and the Templars on his left flanks. After a short battle Richard was victorious and inflicted many losses in Saladin's army. With reports from England that he was urgently advised to return home he was finally forced to negotiate a truce with Saladin, in 1192. This became known as the Treaty of Jaffa. By this treaty, Richard, on behalf of the Christian forces, was given the lands along the coast between Tyre and Jaffa. Jerusalem and the Holy Places were omitted. This arrangement was a disaster for the Templars. They could no longer protect pilgrims travelling to the Holy Places but had to confine themselves to the defence of the narrow strip of land granted by the Truce. Thus, one of the primary objectives of the Templars, the protecting of pilgrims on their way to the Holy Places and Jerusalem, was removed. Eventually, King Richard commenced his long journey home. Even though he was dressed in a Templar habit to avoid recognition, he and his four Templar companions were taken prisoner by the Duke of Austria and held for a ransom of 150,000 marks. Taxes had to be raised again in England so that his freedom could be secured. After languishing in prison for a few years he was finally released. It is said that the Templars paid more than half of the ransom money. Richard died in 1199 and was succeeded by his brother John who had claimed the throne during his absence. During the following turbulent times in England, the Templars supported whoever was on the throne but later helped to preserve the throne for young Henry III. It was during the reign of Henry III that the Templars' influence reached its peak in the English Court.

The Fall of Acre

Shortly after the departure King Richard for England, Saladin died. He was succeeded by Baybar who became leader of the Mamaluk forces. He had come to power by assassinating the Sultan Kutuz who had defeated the Mongols south of Nazareth. Baybar died in 1177 and was succeeded by his commander Qalawun who died on his way to attack Acre. He was replaced by his son, Al-Ashraf as head of the Mameluk forces. Despite the fact that the defenders of Acre had six months notice of the intention of the Mameluks to attack the city, little was done to improve the fortifications or seek help from the West.

The combined forces of Al-Ashraf from Syria and Egypt with over 100 siege-engines, giant catapults and mangonels arrived outside of Acre but did not begin the siege until the arrival of Al-Ashraf himself on the fifth of April 1291. Inside the walls of the city were over 1,000 knights, 14,000 soldiers and about 40,000 inhabitants. Each able bodied man was obliged to man the long walls and battlements. On the morning of the sixth of May the attack commenced with a bombardment of the city by catapults and mangonels. Showers of arrows darkened the sky as the Mameluk forces moved forwards to try and undermine the walls. With every attack it soon became obvious to the defenders that they had inadequately trained soldiers on the walls. When one of the towers was breached it was set on fire and the defenders abandoned that part of the walls.

By the fifteenth most of the towers had been taken and things were looking grim. At this stage, William of Beaujeu, the Templar Master, led out his knights in a counter attack but he was repulsed and driven back inside the walls. He died later from the wounds he sustained. The same fate befell the Hospitaller Master, Matthew of Clermont. Seriously wounded he was transferred to one of the Hospitaller ships in the harbour. Panic set in and everyone tried to get aboard ship and escape the Muslims. People even tried to swim out to the nearby vessels at anchor hoping to be picked up. Roger de Flor, who was in command of a Templar ship and whose activities as a pirate were mentioned in an earlier chapter, demanded money from those who wished to embark.

By nightfall the city was cut off from the harbour as the Muslims took over all exit routes. The Mameluks killed thousands and took many women and young girls as slaves. The only place to remain in Christian hands was the Templar fortress near the sea. Due to its position the fortress was able to be supplied with food and water from the galleys. It became obvious to Al-Ashraf that the stronghold could not be taken so a peace was proposed.

A number of Mameluks were allowed into the fortress with their Emir. They immediately began to assault the women and were attacked and killed by the enraged Templars. Seeing that the situation would get more desperate, Peter de Sevrey ordered the transfer of all the Templar treasure and relics to one of their ships in the harbour. He decided to remain on with a small number of knights. Having been guaranteed safe conduct he went to Al-Ashraf's tent where they were all restrained and beheaded. A few days later, the Mameluks breached one of the walls of the fortress and killed everyone found inside. Meanwhile, Theobald Gaudin, the new Grand Master of the remaining Templars sailed from Sidon to Cyprus with the treasures of the Order while another group of Templars sailed up the coast to the island of Ruad where they remained for the following twelve years. The presence of Christian forces in the Holy Land had finally come to an end and the Templar role had terminated at a terrible cost of lives.

The fall of Acre in May 1291 was the final blow to the Templars. They had suffered the loss of their main base along with most of their fighting men and equipment. The fortress had been deemed impregnable but the Mameluks succeeded in breaching the walls at a number of places. Acre had been a visible sign of the military strength of the Templars. In

A tower at Acre today

Cyprus, the Templars felt ill at ease as the Hospitallers had already set up their base on the island to continue to care for the sick and infirm. The Templars, however, had nothing to do but to partly return to a monastic life as their main *raison d'etre* had been removed.

With no possibility of reclaiming Jerusalem and the Holy Land from the Muslims and with all the Christians having fled from Palestine and another Crusade out of the question, the two main objectives or purposes of the Order's existence were no more. The Templars had fought with valour in the Holy Land and elsewhere and many of its brotherhood had lost their lives. One estimate of those Templars who had fallen in the Middle East gives a figure of 20,000.

Many commentators blame the long-running feud between the Templars and the Hospitallers for the loss of the Holy Land. In fact, the quarrels between them were the cause of losing many battles such as that of Ptolemais in 1291. The popes tried to unite both Orders but without success. The Templars did not wish to declare the riches that they had accumulated or to share these with the Hospitallers and were completely against the idea.

Their pride prevailed over all suggested changes and it aroused the hatred of many enemies or opponents. Their privileges were looked at with envy by the secular clergy as the Templars had become a law unto themselves. They were now a strong rich corporation of men who had lost their high ideals. They were no longer fighting a war against the Muslims so their riches could no longer be excused They were now but a company which had become bankers to popes, kings, nobles and the common people. They even subsidised those in conflict so that at the end they would accrue more wealth for themselves.

* * *

In 1292, the Grand Master of the Templars, Thibaud Gaudin, who had safely removed all the Templar treasures from Acre to Cyprus, died from old age. He was succeeded by James de Molay who went to Rome to meet Pope Boniface VIII. He then journeyed to France and England to seek assistance for another crusade but both kings were in a dispute over territory in France.

Also, at that time a dispute arose between Philip IV of France and Boniface regarding the king's right to tax the clergy. Their disagreement continued and the pope was accused of being elected by treachery, that he was a sodomite and that he didn't believe that the French had souls. The main instigator of these accusations was one, William de Nogaret, who had become Philip's close advisor. These types of false accusations were to be brought into play again later against the Templars by Philip when Bernard de Got became pope.

The relationship between Boniface and Philip became so acrimonious that Boniface was seriously considering the excommunication of Philip when William de Nogaret and Sciarra Colonna, the pope's enemy from Spain, arrived at the papal court at Anagni with an army to arrest him. The pope was rescued by the citizens of the city but died shortly afterward, probably of shock.

Boniface was succeeded by Benedict VIII who tried to sort out the problem but he died within eight months before the matter was resolved. Using the name, of Clement V, Bertrand de Got, Archbishop of Bordeaux became the next pope. Being a close friend of King Philip he accepted the offer that he could set up the papacy in Avignon as he was afraid of his life in Rome which was in civil turmoil. The papacy remained in Avignon until 1378.

In 1304, the then Master of the Templars, James de Molay, eager to begin another crusade summoned William de More,

Jacques (James) De Molay, from a nineteenth century lithograph

Master of the English Temple, to discuss the possibility of getting help from King Edward I of England. The king declined on the excuse that he had to quell the uprising in Scotland. The king of France also made his excuses. Pope Clement V summoned the Masters of the Temple and the Hospitallers to his court in Avignon in order to consider the possibilities of a new crusade. Before the matter was discussed the pope suggested that both Orders should be unified. James de Molay angrily rejected such a suggestion knowing full well that the wealth and property of the Templars far exceeded that of the Hospitallers.

Suffering from ill-health, the pope did not push the matter any further. Not until the Templar Order was dissolved and its properties taken over by the Hospitallers did the two orders come together. The lack of effort in regaining the Holy Land was not due to the inactivity of the Templars and Hospitallers, yet without the assistance of the European kings they were helpless. However, due to their apparent inactivity to regain the Holy Land their popularity declined amongst the royal courts and the people.

The tell-tale signs of the decline in support for the military Orders by the various popes began around 1238, when Pope Gregory IX accused the Hospitallers of heresy and ordered them to correct their ways. In the same year his decree *Ad Nostrum* outlawed the beliefs of some lay groups of men and women who had religious houses. These were permitted to continue their religious lives provided that they accepted ecclesiastical authority.

Fearing an upheaval in the church more than anything else Pope Innocent IV, in 1252, licensed the use of torture in cases dealing with heresy. From the thirteenth century onwards the custom of accusing somebody of heresy increased dramatically. As it was almost impossible to escape or deny the charge of heresy, 'heretics' who confessed would often later deny their confessions. These were then handed over to the secular authority and were either condemned to life imprisonment or else burned at the stake. As a further warning to the Templars of what they could expect, the Teutonic Order of Livonia was accused of heresy by its political enemies. An investigation was ordered by the pope but no evidence against that Order was found. The Teutonic Order was a group of crusader knights from Lübeck and Bremen in modern-day Germany. They founded a hospital in Jerusalem under the patronage of Saint Mary of the Germans, to cater for the sick, injured and infirm. Their Order, approved by Pope Celestine III, was formed on the lines of the Hospitallers and adopted the Templar Rules. They also dressed themselves like Templars but had a black cross on their white tunics.

King Philip IV of France found that after the various wars with England his treasury was empty. He had already confiscation all the Jewish properties, taken all their money and banished them from his kingdom. There was a general state of anarchy in his domain and when he was out one day in his carriage he had to seek sanctuary in the Temple in Paris. Seeing the vast amount of wealth he immediately realised that he possibly had a solution to his money problems.

With the accusations against the Templars that they were involved in black-magic, sorcery and necromancy being spread like wildfire around the courts of Europe his confidence grew. As accusations grew, it was wrongly stated that the book of Templar Rules, which was written by Saint Bernard, was a translation of an Arabic magical text. In addition, it was charged that the Templars adored an image of a bearded head and that they behaved like Muslims in blaspheming Jesus Christ and the Virgin Mary. Also, they were accused of using relics to cure men and women.

Those making the accusations, which were becoming more outlandish every day, did not know, in their ignorance, that the other fighting Orders had the same head on their seals and that the Muslims regarded Jesus as a great prophet and believed that his mother was a virgin. In this context, it should be remembered that the majority of the ordinary rank and file of the Templars were secular men with little or no education. If anyone was interested in magic, it would have been the *literati* and these were few in numbers amongst the Templars.

Filled with a burning desire to get his hands on the treasures of gold, silver and priceless ornaments and relics, King Philip journeyed to see the pope in 1305. He tried to convince Clement V that the Templars were conniving to destroy the papacy and the Faith in the West. Regardless of the lack of cooperation from the pope he decided to proceed with his plans to arrest and imprison the Templars. It took two almost two years before the plan was brought into fruition.

As he sought valid excuses to arrest the Templars for heresy, the arrival of Esquiu de Floyran of Beziers, an ex-Templar chaplain, from Spain with a draft of accusations against the Templars was more than welcome. These accusations had been firmly rejected by King James II in Spain but were gladly accepted as fact by Philip, who immediately arranged that Floyran and William de Nogaret should come together and make further drafts of accusations which could be used against the Templars. It was William de Nogaret who came up with the earlier trumped-up charges against Pope Boniface VIII and Bishop Guichard of Troyes.

Philip, meantime, circulated amongst the people that it was his duty as a Catholic king to root our heresy in his kingdom. He even went so far as to consult the learned professors at the University of Paris to see whether he, as king, had the power to arrest the Templars for heresy. They replied that the Templars were a religious Order and as such could not be under the king's jurisdiction. In some quarters they were still regarded as holy and devout people who wanted to be martyrs and to lay down their lives for God. Yet, undaunted, the king, aided by Floyran and de Nogaret, began to make plans for a surprise arrest of all the Templars in his kingdom.

THE TEMPLARS AND IRELAND

According to the official English records the Templars first arrived in Ireland in September, 1220, however, other documentary evidence including a deed signed by Mathew, a Templar, and Lawrence O'Toole in 1177 indicate that the Templars were in Ireland before 1177.

In their Medieval Religious Houses in Ireland both Aubrey Gwynn and R. Neville Hadcock state that the Templar Order was introduced into Ireland before the death of Laurence O'Toole in 1180. It is therefore possible that they came with Prince John on his first visit or earlier.

The Hospitallers or Knights of the Hospital are reputed to have come to Ireland with the first wave of Anglo-Norman knights in 1168 or 1169. Knowing that they were entering a hostile country where they might be attacked they would have been accompanied by those who cared for the injured and sick.

Further evidence is that some of the Hospitallers and Templars had the same surnames, which would indicate that they were related to some of the earliest Anglo-Normans that arrived in Ireland. In fact, it seems likely that the Templars and the Hospitallers arrived with Maurice Fitzgerald, de Lacy, Fitzgilbert and some adventurous knights in 1168 and 1169. It is interesting to note that some of the de Lacys and the Fitzgeralds were Templars prior to this time. One of them, Gilbert de Lacy, is mentioned as having escorted some noble knights to Antioch in 1163.

There are clear indications that they also accompanied Strongbow, who came in the following year as records show that he donated properties around Kilmainham and Clontarf in county Dublin to the Templars and Hospitallers. One of the earliest sources states that the Templars and Hospitallers had over 19 preceptories and 12 establishments in Ireland by 1172 between them.

There is no record of King Henry II of England having granted any property to either Order during his visit to Ireland in 1172. What they did receive initially was land in the vicinity of Waterford, Wexford, Limerick and Dublin. Unfortunately, there is no proper schedule of lands that originally belonged to the Templars. The first parcels of land included in these grants were areas at Clontarf and Crook. In addition there is a deed listed in the Chartulary of Saint Mary's Abbey dated 1185 and signed by Giraldus Cambrensis and Walter, the Templar of Clontarf.

Other grants soon followed and included the marsh near Waterford, situated between the king's house and the sea, plus lands belonging to the de Lacys and Montfichets. They also received mills at Wexford and Waterford and

Henry I of England

later lands in Carlow, Louth, Kilkenny, Sligo and many other locations where they built houses or preceptories.

By 1308 their Irish lands were worth over £400 per annum and were one of the most productive source of income in all of Europe. The existing tenants on the lands, which came into their possession were Irish. They had to plough the lands, plant crops, create pastures, cut down trees and clear wooded areas. The right to cut down the forests was a special privilege granted by the English king at that time. The tenants were usually paid in goods or in kind for their work but in later years were paid either one or two pennies per week.

There is no record that the master of the Templars in Ireland had a fixed abode, but all indications are that it must have been in Dublin at Clontarf, as the different masters acted as advisors or filled some other high office for the king in Dublin. The Templar master was, in fact, an officer of the English Crown and one of the auditors of the Irish exchequer together with the prior of the Hospitallers. Sometimes, he acted as mediator in disputes between the Anglo-Normans and the Irish chiefs and later between the Anglo-Irish and the Plantagenets. In England, similar duties were carried out for the Crown Treasury.

When not engaged in the king's work, the Irish master travelled around the country visiting all the Templar's establishments and holdings. During these visits preceptors or others in charge made their reports, important business was discussed, property transferred or promotions made of some member to a vacant office. It was also an opportunity of accepting new members into the Order.

The master was also obliged to travel to London at least once a year to make a full report to the English Master of the Temple at which time the proceeds of the various estates were handed over. In the Grant of Henry III the privileges of the Templars were made clear and he gave them immunity from most of the Irish customs i.e. they were exempt from all fines and aids; from all works of castles, parks, bridges and enclosures and from providing carriage for such undertakings; that their woods or corn should not be seized for such work; that they could collect enough wood from their forests for their own use; they were to be free of all tolls at every market, bridge, roadway and sea; also free of tolls for their own markets. If any of the brotherhood lost life or limb for a crime or fled, the criminal's goods should revert to the Order and not to the king. There were also some minor exemptions concerning their tenants.

In addition, King Edward I gave them complete criminal and civil jurisdiction over their tenants and vassals and the power to punish those found guilty of carrying out a criminal act against them. He also gave them the power of trying criminals by ordeal including the use of the pit and the gallows. They were also free from all military duties and Irish feudal customs. This freedom led to a certain amount of abuse by both the Templars and the Hospitallers. The result of these abuses was that the local clergy made many representations to the king. Even the pope was alerted by the Irish bishops and Church Synods that the Templars were misusing and extending their privileges. They, together with the Hospitallers, were reprimanded for abusing the privilege of trying criminals which was normally solely the right of the king's Court.

There is very little on record as to the administration of the Templars in Ireland except that the Irish Master was the head of the Order in Ireland. He and the rest of his Brethren were subject to the Master of the Temple in England. The Irish Master was elected by a General Chapter of the English branch of the Order. Some English sources relate that the king had some influence on the election of who was to become the Irish Master. It was generally accepted that the Master was elected for life but it is recorded that both Peter de Malvern and William de Warnye were elected only for a number of years as can be seen on the List of Masters in the next chapter.

The administration of the Templars in Ireland was as follows – under the Master came the preceptors who were responsible for the management of the manors and estates of the Order. The Master and the preceptors were obliged to travel to London to assist at the English General Chapter of the Order. Each of the preceptors had a chaplain to administer the sacraments to the preceptory members. Following the chaplains came the *fratres servientes* (brother servants) who were also called *armigeri* (men-at-arms) whose purpose was to defend the possessions of the Order from aggression and to be ready to travel to the Holy Land. After the fall of Acre their only duty was to protect the preceptories in Ireland from the rebellious Irish Clans. These *fratres servientes* were not always of noble blood but of the citizen class.

Below these came another group who were also called *fratres servientes* or *famuli* who performed menial jobs like farming and household works. In addition, the Order had free tenants (*firmarii* and *betagii*) on their lands who were obliged to give a certain amount of free days working the Templar lands during the year. Also, there were parcels of land donated to the Templars and these were looked after by stewards who reported to the nearest preceptor. At their preceptories the Templars held manor courts and also ecclesiastical courts at which a canonist sat and dispensed justice. Holding manor courts gave them the same privileges as feudal lords.

On a number of occasions the Templars were assessed to provide members-at-arms for the protection of the country which would mean the king's domain of Ireland and England. However, the Templars quoted that they were free from such service by earlier Royal Grants. As for the king's request for assistance in the war against the Scots it is not known if the Templars participated like the Knights of Saint John (Hospitallers) who were not bound by the rule of not participating in battle against other Christians. The Templars left few documents of their time in Ireland despite the fact that they were in the midst of almost continuous warfare between the Irish, the Anglo-Normans and the Crown. There are no records of any skirmishes, battles or encounters with the native Irish. The activities of the Irish chieftains before and after the Vikings are fairly well recorded including their pillage and plunder of the main monasteries where gold and silver were stored. Yet, there is no mention of attacks on Templar or Hospitaller houses.

It seems that the Templars kept to themselves and were busy elsewhere in legal contests. The records of the English occupation at that time are full of entries of cases which involved the knights, like the right of presentation to churches, pleas for land, and disputes over certain ownerships. The records give details of the appointments of lawyers for both parties and full accounts of the proceedings, such as a dispute over the presentation of one party or another to a vacant church or a dispute between the Templars and the local Bishops regarding lands.

Just to mention a few cases: there is one where the Master of the Templars was accused, by the jurors of Co. Kildare, of having no horses at Kilcork for the defence of the Realm. In the circumstances, he was not bound to have horses as the Order was exempt from such services. A somewhat similar case arose in Dublin, in 1302 when livestock of the Templars was taken and sold by the agents of the Sheriff. The plea was that the Templars had failed to supply horses and men-at-arms. The preceptor of Clontarf argued that he and his predecessors had always been free from such a service due to Royal Charter. Judgement was given in the Templar's favour and the agents were fined.

Another interesting case was the one in which a Matilda de Botillere brought a case against the Master of the Templars who objected to her presenting a fit person to the vicarage of Carlingford. The Master produced a deed by which a Matilda de Lacy (probably mother or ancestor) had granted to the Templars the lands at Coly and the right of nominating the vicar. But there was a rectory as well as a vicarage attached to the church and Matilda argued that the Templars were only given the rectory. The judge ruled against Maltilda and the archbishop of Armagh was ordered to accept a fit person presented by the Templars. Matilda was fined six marks for wasting the court's time. There were many other cases in session or pending when it was announced that the Templars were being imprisoned and their goods being seized.

Henry was succeeded by Stephen on his death, despite the fact that Henry's daughter, Matilda, was named heiress to the throne. Stephen was chosen as king by the barons and citizens of London instead of Henry's daughter. The result was civil war in England. Stephen was described as a generous and affable man, a good commander in war and a man of the people. According to the Inquest of 1185 the Templars received some 37 grants of land from Stephen and his supporters while Matilda made 11 grants to the Order.

During the reign of Matilda's son, Henry II, the number of grants doubled. Amidst this confusion and civil war between the forces of Stephen and Matilda the Templars did not get involved in the dispute for the Crown. They were busy setting up their preceptories and houses while the forces of

Matilda and Stephen fought each other. This was the period when the Templars gained most of their lands and properties in Ireland. When Henry II came to power he granted the Templars in Ireland and England annual alms of one mark from the proceeds of every Sheriff's possession.

The conditions under which the Templars had to live in Ireland were similar to those in England except that they were surrounded by hostile tribes or clans in some regions. Those living in the countryside far from Dublin had to fortify their preceptories or houses. Like other Anglo-Normans they built a number of castles or fortified houses. Being far removed from London, which was the centre of the Templar operations in the British Isles, the Irish Master and the brothers had more freedom and were not subject to the secular clergy or ecclesiastical authority.

During their period in Ireland two of the Masters fell into temptation, namely, Ralph of Southwark and Walter Bachelor. Little is known abut the transgressions of Ralph of Southwark but Walter Bachelor was excommunicated for stealing Templar property. He was removed to the Temple in London where he was tortured and held in a small penitential cell where he died. His death at the Temple was one of the subjects brought up during the inquisition. Those present at the London Temple at the time of his death declared that he had died from natural causes but all indications are that he died from torture.

In 1220 the government of Henry III gave instructions to the English Viceroy (Justiciar) of Ireland that all taxes, duties and income from Ireland should be handed over to the Templars and Hospitallers as they would be held responsible for the safe keeping and transfer to the Royal coffers at London. This arrangement was identical to their duties in England. Henry also gave instructions to the archbishop of Dublin, the Chief Judiciary of Ireland, and the Irish Master of the Knights Templars that a copy of the proceeds of all duties etc. be sent to him and that Templars should themselves transfer the monies to the English exchequer.

The Templars at this time were held in high respect by Henry, whose advisor, almoner and official was a Templar called Brother Geoffrey. In Ireland, about this time, Brother Ralph of Southward was apprehended. He had been Master of the Temple in Ireland. He was replaced by a Brother Roger le Waleis who audited the accounts of Ireland together with the Archdeacon of Dublin and Maurice Fitzgerald who was the Chief Justiciary. The Templars also became involved in the collection of new customs duties including those of Waterford. During this period – 1254 to 1260 – King Henry confiscated all the Jewish property in his kingdoms and levied dues on all monasteries including those of the Templars. In order to raise further money, the heads of each monastic Order could buy back their Privileges by the payment of £150. It is not known if this levy of dues extended to the properties of the Templars in Ireland.

While the Templars were involved in financial matters, the Hospitallers were allotted military posts and were required to take up arms like the Welsh and Anglo-Norman knights. The Master (Prior) of the Hospitallers in Ireland usually took command. All religious houses of the Templars and the Hospitallers that were established in the country were required to be fortified, if necessary, against attacks by the Irish chieftains. It was well known that some of the Irish chieftains plundered the old religious establishments for booty and anything of value. The Templars did not take part in any military activity against the Irish chieftains as they were bound by the Rules of their Order not to engage in warfare against other Christians unless they were attacked.

In 1298, King Edward I of England summoned the English and Irish Templars to join his forces in the struggle against William Wallace of Scotland. In the defeat of Wallace and his army at Falkirk, Brian De Jay, Master of the Hospitallers in England, was killed.

In the fourteenth century, the Hospitallers found it impossible but to assist in military campaigns of the king. Edward obliged the Masters of the Hospital in both England and Scotland to pay him

Edward I of England, from a nineteenth century drawing

homage as they were not required to pay the Crown any levies or duties on their property according to the privileges bestowed on them by various popes. This practice was also followed by the king of France and other minor monarchs in Europe. The support of the European Christian kings was vital to the Military Orders in their struggle in the East. To join the Crusades was a source of prestige and glory for the nobles and knights. That is if they came back alive.

As in England the Templars in Ireland received various legal privileges which included a partial exemption of their tenants from royal jurisdiction. They were, in addition, allowed to carry on trading and to transport their goods to ports for export without paying duties. They were also exempt from the traditional duties such as shield tax, tallage (toll on tenants of Crown property and towns) and castle guard. However, the Templars gradually fell out of favour with the English Crown from about 1250 and the Hospitallers took over their important positions. The Templars received fewer donations and gifts from the king. This royal action was also followed in Ireland where the Hospitallers were given all the important administrative, financial and military posts. What brought about this change is rather vague. Maybe it was because the Hospitallers were considered better administrators as they were continuously being joined by more suitable recruits or because the Templars concentrated more on raising donations and money for the Holy Land.

Henry III slowly began to regard the Military Orders, especially the Templars, as obstructive and difficult to work with. Also, he was of the opinion that they had received too much property and too many privileges and might eventually be powerful and proud enough to undermine his royal authority so he nominated a number of Hospitallers to their places in the royal court.

As was the case in European mainland cities, the Templars in the British Isles had a number of quarters ('frank-houses') in the cities which were used by visitors and travellers who paid a charge per night. This was one of the means by which the Templars raised additional money. In fact at first, they had numerous quarters in each city which were exempt from tithes. These were marked or identified by placing a red timber cross on the door. When other house owners took advantage of the situation by placing red crosses on their own properties to confuse the Crown collectors and escape paying tithes this was recognised as abuse by the king's advisors and the Templars were then limited to one hostel in both Waterford and Dublin. In Limerick, this directive did not seem to be followed as the records show that the Templars retained a number of houses.

The Templars were engaged in the raising of sheep and the export of wool to England and the Continent. They produced a surplus of corn and this together with wheat was exported to England. One thing of note in this context is that the Templars seemed to have been engaged in the breeding of good horses which were probably destined for sale in Europe or maybe to sell to the king's knights in England or France.

In total, each preceptory in Ireland had an annual income valued at over £25 which could only be compared to those in Northumberland properties.

Henry II of England
from a manuscript illustration

They also had a number of mills including those at Waterford and Kilsaran in Co. Louth. These were used to crush their own wheat and corn as well as that of their tenants and neighbours. They were protected by 'the milling soke' whereby tenants were obliged to use the mills of their lords (Templars). This was also a good source of revenue for the Templars. A number of mills were included in grants to the Templars in a Charter of Henry II. Later, the express instructions of Henry III forbade the construction of any mill in Waterford and elsewhere that would be in opposition to those of the Templars. Other Templar mills in the country were similarly protected.

As mentioned earlier the corn and produce of the lands of the Templars was more that enough to feed themselves and their servants. In 1213, King John of England permitted the Templars to export their own wool. And in 1225, King Henry III granted a licence for five years to the Irish Master of the Templars to sell his wheat and corn etc. throughout

Ireland without paying any dues etc. Later, in 1294, when King Edward I ordered the confiscation of all goods of the merchants and subjects of the king of France, the Templars bought most of these goods. It is noted that the Master, Walter le Bachelor, paid the king's treasury about £230. (See Receipt Roll of 1295). No doubt, these goods were later sold on at a nice profit. In fact, Walter le Bachelor, was soon afterwards excommunicated and transported to the London Temple where he died. He was found guilty of selling off goods and property of the Templars in Ireland. Later during the inquisition the cause of his death was investigated as rumours abounded that he was tortured and placed in a small cell at the Temple.

* * *

Nationality of the Templars in Ireland

After an examination of the main sources it is evident that some Irish did, in fact, join the Templars. The knights were originally Anglo-Normans or Franks of noble blood and governed by the English Master in London.

In Plea Rolls No.76 there is a reference to a number of *servientes* (servants of knights) of the preceptory at Clonaul being of Irish origin. It is probable that these new recruits did accompany the knights who went to the Holy Land from Ireland on Crusade.

It is recorded that groups of Templars departed this country for Palestine on the third Crusade as the pope issued orders to the archbishop of Dublin that he was not to demand money (collection for Crusade) from those Templars in Ireland going to the Holy Land as they were exempt from the Constantinople Subvention. The main object of the Templars was to make the best use of the properties granted to them by the various kings of England so that these could generate enough money to sustain their brothers who were fighting in the Holy Land.

* * *

Status of Templars in Ireland

Ireland and Scotland were part of the Templar province of England. The size and location of each province was dictated by language. Thus, the main provinces were in England, France, Northern Spain, Italy, and the Middle East. In Ireland all the Masters were elected by the English general chapter at the London Temple from amongst the English Brethren. In his History of the Viceroys, Sir John Gilbert stated that, in 1274, Guillaume FitzRoger, the Master of the Knights of the Temple in Ireland was taken prisoner and a number of his companions were killed in battle fighting against the Irish at Glenmalure. This information was incorrect as Guillaume FitzRoger was in fact the Prior of the Hospitallers at Kilmainham, Dublin.

With a substantial amount of the country under Anglo-Norman dominance, settlers and adventurers came to Ireland. The Church was reorganised into parishes which were subject to tithes. In addition to the Templars and the Hospitallers the Anglo-Normans made many grants of property to the other Orders including the Augustinians and the Franciscans to build many monasteries. The Templars, on the other hand built small houses. Some of these did not even have a chapel and the main hall acted as a place of worship, chapter room and refectory. It is estimated that only one or two brothers at the most stayed in these houses and the head brother was responsible to the nearest preceptor. The cultivation of the land and the raising of farm stock were the main prerogatives

Key to Ireland Map

A1.... Ainy	K1.... Kilbride
A2.... Askeaton	K3.... Kilcloggan
A3.... Ardfinnan	K4.... Kilsaran
B1.... Baldungan	K5.... Kilcork
B2.... Ballintemple	R1.... Rathbride
C1.... Clontarf	R2.... Rincrew
C2.... Crooke	R3.... Rathronan
C3.... Clonaulty	T1.... Templetown

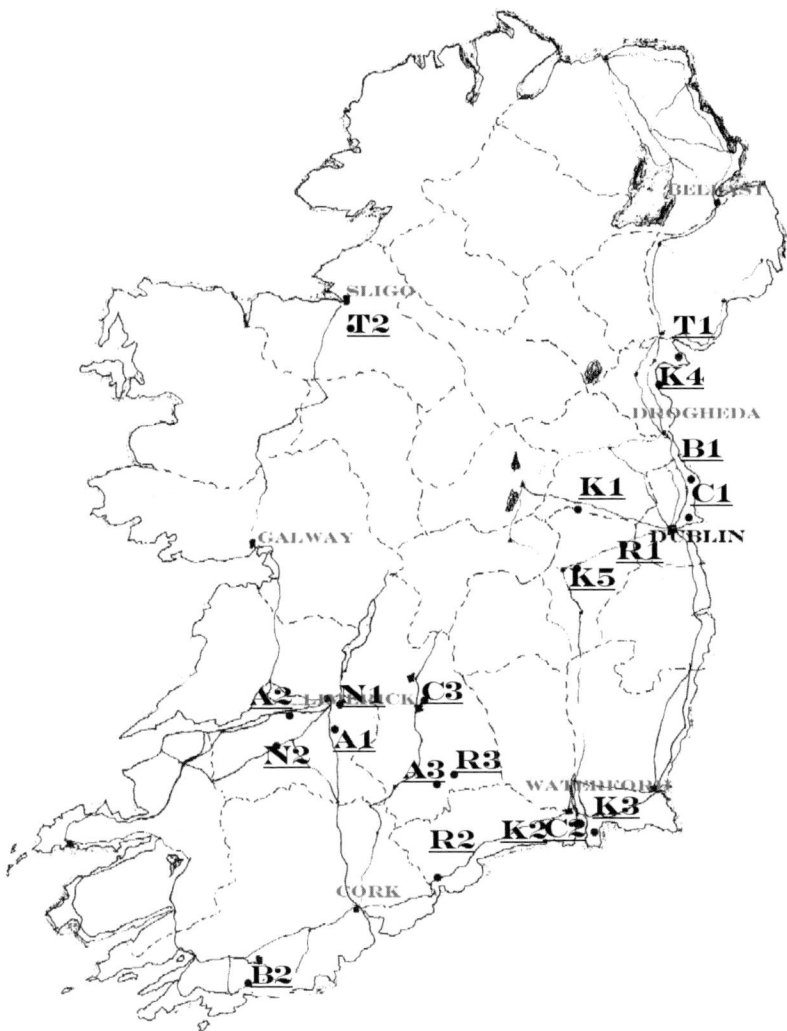

Some of the major Templar holdings in Ireland

of the Templars. No doubt, there were many squabbles and confrontations with the native Irish concerning the use of 'commonages.' It is not known how the native Irish regarded the Templars. They were probably seen in the same way as the other monastic Orders, like the Augustinians and Cistercians, but as people who kept to themselves. There are no records of any serious confrontation between the Irish and the Templars. It is said, that as far as Irish history is concerned, the Templars never existed except when they were arrested and their goods and lands confiscated.

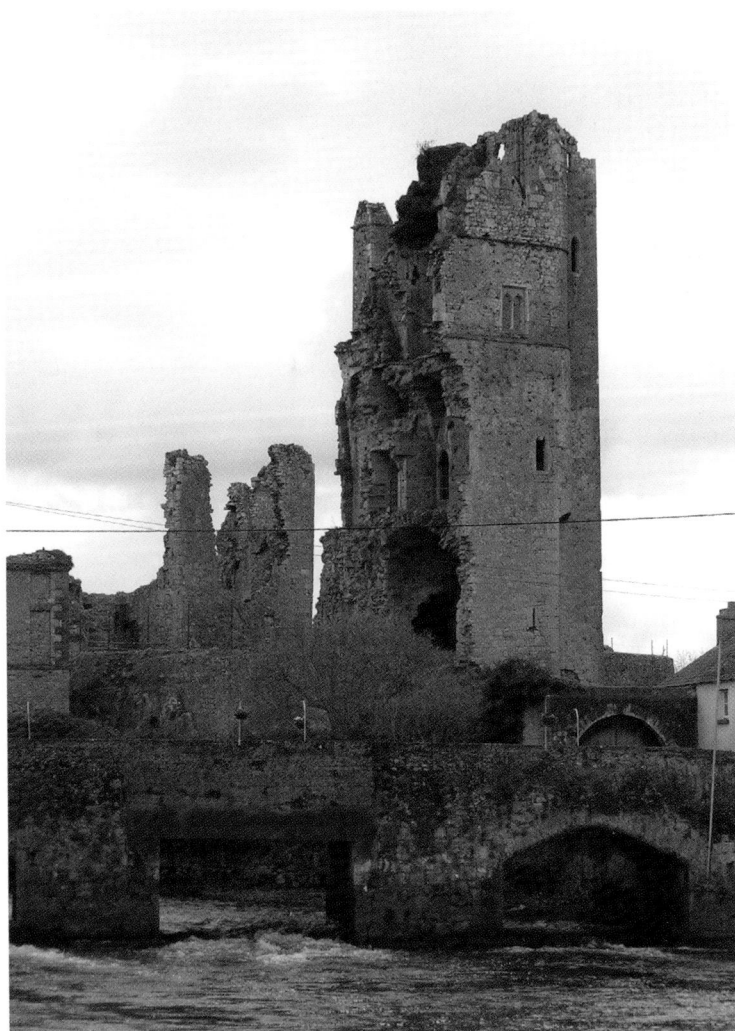

Askeaton, possible site of a Templar Commandery

Ballingarry Castle

The Templars in Ireland

As most of the following have English or Anglo-Norman surnames they must have been elected from the brotherhood in England. There is no record of any Irish becoming a full member of the Order except for a vague reference that Diarmuid, fourth son of the Earl of Desmond was a Master. Some of these Templars were later arrested and tried, while others later gave evidence against their own brothers. These had already been dismissed from the Order.

1180	Walter the Templar
	Guarnerus
1200–1210	Hugh the Templar
1210	Henry Foliot
1234	Ralph de Southwark
1235–50	Roger le Waleis
1257–73	Herbert de Mancester
1258–88	Roger de Glastonbury
1288	Thomas de Toulouse
1295–1301	Walter le Bachelor
(Excommunicated for selling off Templar lands)	
1300–1308	Peter de Malvern
1302–1306	William de Waryne
1307–1308	Henry Tanet

Irish castles, houses and lands originally belonging to Templars

No schedule of lands that originally belonged to the Templars exists today. There are many locations which either by tradition or noted by some historians have been described as Templar properties. It is possible that in some cases lands that originally belonged to the Templars before the suppression of the Order had been assigned to other parties during the 20 years or so before they were handed over to the Hospitallers and no record of these exchanges remain today. Much of this confusion is further increased by people mixing up the Knights of the Temple and the Knights of Saint John in historical works. There may have been occasions when certain tracts of land had been exchanged, granted away or held free of rent from the lord of the area, but these are minor. In this work the majority of places mentioned in various sources have been examined as to ascertain whether they had been Templar property or not.

Firstly, the following is a list of the preceptories located in Ireland according to Hore. This seems to be just a basic list of the main houses situated near or on the east coast of Ireland. The chief manor of the Templars was more than likely at Clontarf and not Kilmainham as believed by many. Many of their preceptories or manors in the countryside consisted of a church, house and outhouses. Some were fortified as castles to protect the occupants from attacks by the Irish Clans. In the beginning, the native Irish were excluded from joining the Order but amongst the list of seventeen names mentioned regarding Clonoulty, a number of Irish names appear (*see Plea Roll, 33/34 Edw.I.m.27*). According to MacInery there were sixteen Templar foundations (preceptories) together with Clontarf but he stated that the establishments of the

Templars were veiled in secrecy. After detailed research this number appears to have been a minimal estimation as the following lists verify.

Templar Preceptories in Ireland

The preceptories were the main houses of the Templars in certain localities and served as a base for other minor houses where the brothers came together to make their reports on the various holdings. They also served as recruiting and training centres for new members and as places of retirement for the old members who had seen service fighting in the Middle East. Most preceptories had land which was used either for crops or grazing of livestock to support the Order. A few had hospices or hospitals for the poor, sick and infirm. With leprosy prevalent in Ireland about this time many establishments were required for those suffering from this disease and it was mainly the Hospitallers and the Templars with their experience in the East who took up the challenge of looking after those sufferers. The large number of Irish townlands called 'lobhrach' or containing that word will give an indication of the prevalence of leprosy in Ireland during the Middle Ages.

There are seven sites that can fairly confidently be said to have been preceptories but it must be remembered that they may not have all fulfilled this function throughout the whole history of the order in Ireland.

CLONAULTY	KILCLOGGAN
CLONTARF	KILSARAN
CROOK	TEMPLE HOUSE
KILBARRY	

CLONAUL(TY), County Tipperary

This property of the Templars was founded before 1200. It was located north west of Cashel and south of Thurles near the River Suir. Described as a castle but also as a preceptory in the Inquisition into the Templars. Amongst the holding here were four churches which were under the control of the Templars. One of these churches was in dispute as to its advowson by the Templars and the Prior of Athassel who were Augustinian canons and which was situated near Cashel at the time of the suppression of the Order. The castle and lands reverted to the Crown after the Templar arrests but retained the Templar interest. It was later taken over by the Hospitallers who had an establishment nearby.

In the locality is an ancient well known as St John's well.

CLONTARF, County Dublin

This was the main preceptory or commandery of the Templars in Ireland.

The lands, where the main preceptory of the Templars was situated, were granted to the Templars by Henry II. This property as well a church and a mill were located on the north side of Dublin Bay and was the richest of the Templar properties in Ireland.

In 1310 the property and lands were granted to Richard de Burgo, Earl of Ulster, by King Edward. As these do not appear in the Inquisition of his properties after his death it can be assumed that they were handed over to the Hospitallers after the dissolution of the Templars in 1314. Richard or his heirs in a Chapter of 1333 allocated the preceptories of Clontarf, Kilsaran and Castleboy to Prior Outlawe of Kilmainham (Hospitaller). Later, parts of the land were leased out in the middle of the fifteenth century. The buildings listed in 1541 consisted of a hall, two towers, a kitchen and outhouses

The present castle is reputed to have been built by the Netterville family. Its Gothic windows give it a semi-ecclesiastical appearance. Nothing remains today of the old Templar establishment. It is possible that some of the stones of the original building were used in the construction of the later mock gothic castle.

CROOKE (Crook), Co. Waterford

This was a Manor House and had substantial lands of about 450 acres. It was situated in the Barony of Gaultier, County Waterford and happened to be the location where Henry II landed in Ireland in 1172. The property is located some six miles SE of Waterford near the remains of a castle which was built in the late thirteenth century by the Baron of Curraghmore and handed over to the Knights Templar by king Henry II c.1180. Its ownership by the Templars was confirmed by successive kings. There was a protracted law case regarding a section of these lands between the Templars and the Abbot of Dunbrody which was a Cistercian establishment in Wexford. (*see entry for Kilbride below*)

During the period that the Templars were imprisoned in Dublin Castle, the manor of Crook was one of the houses which had to provide sustenance and goods to the Templars.

It subsequently became the property of the Hospitallers after the dissolution of the Templars.

KILBARRY, County Waterford

This property is situated south-west of Waterford, near the coast and close to Kill and Knockmahon.

According to Lewis the Templars had a preceptory and a church in this parish which was founded in the twelfth century. The chapel was dedicated to Saint Antoine. There were still ruins to be seen c.1800.

Originally, the lands were given to the Templars by a charter of King Henry II. The Templars were later granted a lease of adjoining lands by John de Monfichet on payment of five marks (two-thirds of a pound) per annum and a pair of furred gloves or two shillings to the Crown. The property at Kilbarry was a substantial one, the farm being about 300 acres.

The preceptory, buildings and lands were handed over to the Hospitallers c. 1320, well after the dissolution of the Templar Order. In 1322 the Hospitallers were still held responsible for the furnishing of gloves according to the conditions of the old lease to the Templars. In 1327, William de Fyncham was Hospitaller Master of both Kilbarry and Crooke.

The preceptory consisted at least of a house which was connected to a chapel. The ancient well near this site is dedicated to Saint Bernard.

KILCLOGGAN, County Wexford

This was a preceptory of the Templars and was also known as Templetown.

Probably founded by Connor O'Moore between 1183 and 1200, it was situated on the east side of Waterford Harbour. The adjoining townland is called Templetown and Templetown Bay is close by and the property also included a church.

The preceptory was established here during the reign of King John. It was one of the Templar properties chosen by the king to sustain the Templars while they were imprisoned. Some time after the suppression of the Order, during the reign of King Edward II, it became a commandery of the Knights Hospitallers under the prior, Fitzdavid. By 1860 all that remained of the foundation was a tower, which was connected by a corridor to the nineteenth century church. There were no other ruins visible except the nearby Kilcloghan castle.

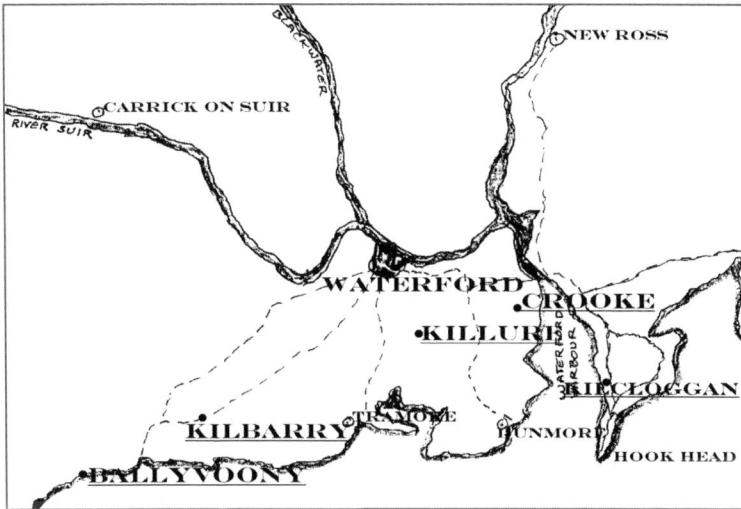

Waterford area with Templar properties underlined

KILSARAN, County Louth (Preceptory and Manor)
This preceptory of the Templars was situated south of
Dundalk town, near castle Bellingham and beside Dundalk
Bay. The original property was donated to the Templars by
Matilda de Lacy and was founded in the twelfth century
about the same time as Cooley. Matilda was the daughter
of Hugh de Lacy, the second Earl of Ulster and a very pious
lady. She was married to Leceline de Verdon. Their daughter
was also called Matilda and she married David, baron of
Naas. Matilda de Lacy's great-grandfather, Gilbert de Lacy,
had become a Templar and had figured as a brave knight in
the East and is portrayed in the records as one of the Templar
knights escorting a group of pilgrim through Turkey.

The property of some 272 acres included a substantial
preceptory with chamber, hall, cellar, kitchen, bake house,
granary and a church. Nothing remains today.

Little has been recorded of the lives and the activities of the
Templars at Kilsaran except when there were disputes about

fishing rights and actions against the Order by local bishops regarding advowson of certain churches.

At the time of the arrests and seizure of properties, which were carried out by sheriff, Benedict le Hauberge and his bailiffs. Only a Brother Hugh was in occupation at Kilsaran at that particular time. He witnessed the inventory taken by the authorities. Anything of value, including chalices, vestments and goblets, were removed to the Chancellor of Ireland in Dublin.

There were ten churches and seventeen parishes under the jurisdiction of the Manor including Drogheda together with their income, tithes and first fruits. In the manor chapel there were three sets of vestments yet there were only two beds, two robes and two horses. Like other possessions of the Templars the manor and lands were farmed out to 'trustworthy' individuals.

All the goods and chattels which were removed from the manor vanished and those who took over the lands etc. failed to give the due income to the Exchequer in Dublin and summonses were issued against these individuals. Included amongst these was Alexander de Bykenore, who had been the king's treasurer in Ireland.

In 1310, a royal grant was issued giving the manors of Kilsaran and Clontarf to Richard de Burgo, the Red Earl of Ulster. From this time onwards, a Philip de Erdely, who was in possession of Kilsaran would have to pay his rent to de Burgo while the Crown reserved for itself the income from the first fruits of the various churches.

It was noted that in the inquisition on the death of Richard de Burgo into his estates and holdings that Kilsaran is not mentioned but it is does appear in the list of the Hospitallers properties which were taken over following the dissolution of the Templars.

TEMPLE HOUSE, Co. Sligo
Near Ballymote, south of Sligo town

This was also referred to as Teachtemple and Loughnehely which took its name from Lake Awnally located nearby.

One of the few holdings that the Templars possessed in the province of Connaught was near Sligo town and called Temple House. Originally the site was occupied by a castle which was built during the reign of Henry III and which was destroyed in 1271. It was mentioned in the *Annals of Lough Ce* as being in existence in 1270. This area of the country was witness to great turmoil in the late thirteenth century so it is unlikely that the Templars could have maintained a major presence after the loss of the castle. The Templars still retained a church and a house nearby however and in the taxation years of 1302-1306 the estate was referred to as Kellecath or Kilvarnet.

Both the church and the house were transferred to the Fratres Cruciferi of the priory of Rindown where this Order held a house, church and lands. It was one of the few properties that the Hospitallers did not acquire after the dissolution of the Templar Order. For more on the Fratres Cruciferi see the entry for Castledermot.

OTHER TEMPLAR PROPERTIES

There are a number of other locations mentioned in various sources where the Templars had a manor, church, parcel of land or frank-houses (free house for travellers and the poor). Those listed as churches had adjoining land which produced crops or was used for the grazing of livestock. The proceeds of these, including tithes went to those (Templars) who had the advowson (rights of celebrating the sacraments etc.) Some of the following locations have old English spelling which makes it difficult to ascertain the correct parish name. In addition there are names gleaned from lists of those properties taken over by the Knights of the Hospital during period 1314-1323

After the arrest and jailing of the Templars in 1308, their properties were seized by the representatives of the Crown. When the pope requested that all Templar lands were to be handed over to the Knights of the Hospital, King Edward II pretended to accept this directive but had already confiscated them for the Crown. Also, many families who had donated lands to the Templars tried to repossess these. In addition, the local clergy seized the opportunity to claim some of the lands and churches which they thought were rightfully theirs. So, in fact, there were four different parties seeking possession of Templar properties. These could be identified as those who donated the lands in the first place, their heirs, the local clergy and the Crown. This, of course, lead to confusion and created many difficulties for historians in determining which house and lands actually belonged to the Templars before their arrest and the dissolution of the Order. The following list is organised by county and includes houses, castles and properties with a well-established Templar connection and also those which are questionable as to Templar ownership.

– COUNTY CARLOW –

ATHKILTON (Athkiltan/Takelton?)
A manor held by the Templars. Goods, lands and trees were mentioned in certificate *HW.332,364*. The site has not been identified for certain but there is an unidentified 'Abbey' site in the nearby north side of the parish of Gowran, which is in Co. Kilkenny. (*See Gowran*)

BALLY MACWILLIAM-ROE
A Preceptory is said to have been built here by the Templars c.1300. *A.55.* There are no records which would indicate that ruins had been found in this locality.

BALLYMEAN (Ballymoon)
A house etc. enclosed by a high wall which could be described as being so heavily fortified that it could be called a castle.

DUNLECKNEY (Leighlinbridge)
This was the seat of the Kavanagh clan, kings of Leinster in ancient history.
   A Templar preceptory existed here from c.1300 to 1308 when the Templars were arrested and their properties seized. There is no mention of ruins in the 1800s *Lewis.I.584.*

FOTHERD (Grange of Forth)

Also known as Templeton.

From the information available it appears that the Templars had a number of plots of land in this area. These would have been at Fotherd, Rathronan and Athkiltan(Takyltan). From the available records it seems that these lands were, in actual fact, rented out to a third parties as a record of income has been recorded. (*See Patent Role, England, 8 Ed II. pt. I, m. 26*). The lands at Athkiltan contained a large oak wood. Some of the trees were given to an Edmund le Botiller to repair houses on his Ballygaveran estate. Following the dissolution of the Templar Order the lands at Fotherd were rented out at the request of Maud de Clare, Countess of Gloucester to a David de Pembroke instead of being handed over to the Knights Hospitallers. When David of Pembroke was killed in the Scottish Wars his widow received the income from the properties at 'Templeton' on the king's orders.

KILLERIG (Friarstown)

Six miles south-east of Castledermot and about six miles east of Carlow town

Killergy, otherwise known as Killerig or Friarstown was a religious establishment of Saint John the Baptist and was founded by Gilbert de Borard. According to Ware in his Antiquities (*vol ii, p.271*) this preceptory belonged to the Templars. Abbe Mac Geoghegan in his History of Ireland, stated that this preceptory belonged to the Knights Templar and then passed on to the Hospitallers after the dissolution of the Order. However, *RK.152,165*, states that the preceptory was built by the Hospitallers and that the Templars held some land in the adjoining area, granted in 1284. In *Plea Rolls 32, Ed.1*, dealing with county Kildare there is an entry where we find 'that Friar Bernard of the Hospital of Kylergi and Friar Robert of Toly, were fined. Earlier in 1290, there was a charter from the Prior of the Hospitallers to one Henry Marshall of Dublin witnessed by the Master of Killergy. It is very unlikely that the Templars handed over Killergy to the Hospitallers at this time. In addition, the title 'Master' was never used by the Templars for a brother who was in charge of a foundation. It is however recorded that the Templars did have property in this locality and that there were seven rectories and a castle.

According to the records the 'preceptory' of Saint John Baptist was founded by Gilbert de Borard during the reign of King John and was confirmed to the Knights Hospitallers by Pope Innocent III in 1212. There is no mention that this was a Templar foundation and transferred to the Hospitallers after the suppression of the Templars. It seems that the controversy about which Order actually possessed Killerig arises from the fact that Templars were granted some adjoining land in 1284. An Inquisition of 1540 shows that there was a castle in ruins, about 350 acres of land and two rectories (churches) in nearby Kyllargan. In addition, in 1542, it is stated that about 350 acres and seven rectories were seized.

– COUNTY CORK –

BALLINTEMPLE
South-east of Clonakilty near Ring.
The Knights Templar are supposed to have built a fine church here in 1392. However, the Templars were disbanded over 80 years earlier. The date given may be incorrect or else the church should be attributed to the Hospitallers. The church was later handed over to the monks at Gill Abbey. Parts of ruins remained in 1837 as well as a graveyard. The ancient graveyard in a double circular rath can still be seen.

BALLYNOE CASTLE

There are vague references in tradition that this was a Templar foundation. It is said that it was an important ecclesiastical centre with a church, graveyard and other buildings. It was taken over by the Knights Hospitallers c. 1320. There were a number of churches and other important buildings in the area including Ballyknock castle.

BRIDGETOWN ABBEY CASTLE, Fermoy

According to *Healy, p.385*, this could possibly have been a Templar foundation. It was handed over to the Augustinian monks from Newtown Friary, Co. Meath, in 1327. Fitzhugh de Roche is said to have been the founder of this abbey. It was described as a fortified enclosure with an infirmary, church, cloisters etc. The history of this abbey indicates that it was always an Augustinian priory and not a Templar or a Hospitaller foundation.

CAHERKEREEN CASTLE, Kilnamatra

This was the location of a hospital, referred to as the 'Fort of the Medicine.' *Healy.* It was more than likely a Hospitallers foundation and not Templar.

CASTLEVENTRY, East Carberry

Situated about six miles north-north-east of Rosscarbery near Reenascreena and listed in the Annals of the Four Masters. The ancient castle itself was known as Castrum Venit or the Castle of the Winds.

There are ruins of an old church high on a hill enclosed by a retaining wall which measured about 24 feet by 16 feet. Nearby was a graveyard It was originally called Templum Ventrie and is said to have been built by the Templars c. 1298, according to Lewis.

CHRISTCHURCH CASTLE, Cork City

This is referred to as the castellated church of the Knights Templar. *Ref: Healy.p.73 and Cusack.* From the early description it is more than likely that the church, otherwise known as the Church of the Holy Trinity, had a tower of some sort or other. No further information is available.

CLOGHROE CASTLE, Blarney

This was a De Cogan Castle built of sandstone, according to *Healy.46.*

References are vague as to whether this was a Templar foundation or not. The ruins of a castle existed in 1656. Presently, there are no ruins to give any indication if the exact location. The De Cogans leased a section of land containing Cloghroe out to Ralph de Guines who is said to have built the castle on the site of an old lios.

COOLE CASTLE and ABBEY, near Fermoy

These are situated about three miles south-east of Fermoy.

The lands are said to have been donated by the de Barrys to the Templars, who are reported to have built a church and castle here around 1296. (*MSS Smith*). There were two churches but only the ruins of one remains. The architecture is that of the thirteenth century. The castle later became the summer residence of the Bishop of Cloyne. There is no history of the church and lands having been passed over to the Knights Hospitallers.

CORK CITY

There is supposed to have been a hospital or frank-house which was near to that of the White Friars (Dominicans). Probably taken over by the Hospitallers from the Templars after the Suppression of the Order.

COURTBRACK CASTLE, Blarney

This was a castle of the MacCarthys na Mona. Its connection, mentioned by Healy, to the Templars seems incorrect. Any connection it had with a religious Order appears to be that with the Knights Hospitallers and their abbey at Mourne is on the road between Cork and Mallow.

There is no further evidence to this supposed connection with the Templars.

KILCREA CASTLE

Kilcrea is about half way between Cork and Macroom and east of Crookstown.

Near the castle of Kilcrea were located a church and other buildings in ruins. It was called the Cell or Chapel of Crea. Windele stated that the church was founded by the Mac Carthys for the Franciscans in 1465 although there are vague references in tradition that there was originally a Templar foundation in the vicinity.

KILRONAN, near Drinagh

In the parish of Drinagh are the ruins of an old church which was reputed to have been built by the Knights Templar. See: Lewis under Drinagh/Dreeny.

MIDDLETON

This was a large church or abbey which is reputed to have been built by the Knights Templar c. 1298. The stones of the ruins were used to build the present church.

MONANIMY

This site is located in the Blackwater valley between Mallow and Fermoy, and south of Castletownroche.

There is a certain amount of confusion regarding this site. The castle can be found just to the north of Kilavullen village and has been restored in modern times. It perches on a limestone outcrop on the northern bank of the Blackwater. The original construction of the castle dates to the thirteenth century. According to Smith there were four parishes or churches under the rectory of Cleghan or the preceptory of Monanimy. He states that the castle with a number of buildings around it near the preceptory was originally a Hospitaller foundation. (*Smith i.342*). *Cassell iv.392*, states that when the church was rebuilt in 1811 it was on the site of the Hospitallers preceptory and that the castle was originally built by the Templars.

MOURNE ABBEY, (Mallnamony/Monaster de Mona)
Situated on the road between Cork to Mallow.

This was a preceptory of the Knights Templar according to *Healy. p.359*. and according to Smith in his *History of the County and City of Cork*. However, according to Ware it was a Hospitaller foundation and I think he was correct. It was also known as the Monaster de Mona and Ballynamony Abbey. The Master of Mora (Mona) was a witness to a deed signed by the Prior of the Hospitallers and the abbey is listed in the taxation year of 1302 as belonging to the Hospitallers. It is probably correct that Mourne was a preceptory of the Knights of Saint John from the very beginning of its existence. An Alexander de Saint Helena seems to have been the founder and it was not recognised as a monastery by Pope Innocent III in 1212. It is recorded that it was given by charter to the Hospitallers who were instructed to build a strong fortified tower in this location. In 1541 only the ruins of a large church and a number of thatched houses were found on the location.

After suppression of the Templars it was still in the hands of the Hospitallers.

RATHCLARIN, East Carberry

Situated about four and a half miles from Bandon and about two miles north-west of the present church were the ruins of the ancient church of Cloundereen which was reputed to have founded by the Knights Templar.

TEMPLEFAUGHNA

The ruins of a number of ancient buildings still existed in this locality up to recently. It was supposed to have been a house and farm of the Templars. *Cooke.447.*

– COUNTY DUBLIN –

BALDUNGAN

This Templar holding was situated in the Barony of Balrothery, formerly in Co. Dublin but now in modern Fingal. It is near the coast about half-way between Dublin and Drogheda.

There was a Templar preceptory and a church in this parish. The church was dedicated to the Blessed Virgin. It is reputed that it became a priory at a later date and it is said that the nuns threw themselves off the upper floors when the castle was attacked by armed men.

There are still ruins of a church with a tower of ten sides which was not unusual for a Templar edifice. There was also a strong fortress located nearby which was erected in the thirteenth century by the Barnewall family.

The templar castle was of the twelfth century and it passed to the Howth family by marriage sometime in the sixteenth. Like many other Irish castles it was burned by Cromwell's forces in 1641.

BRAY

From the English records of 1284 it appears that the Templars had land and houses rented out in this location

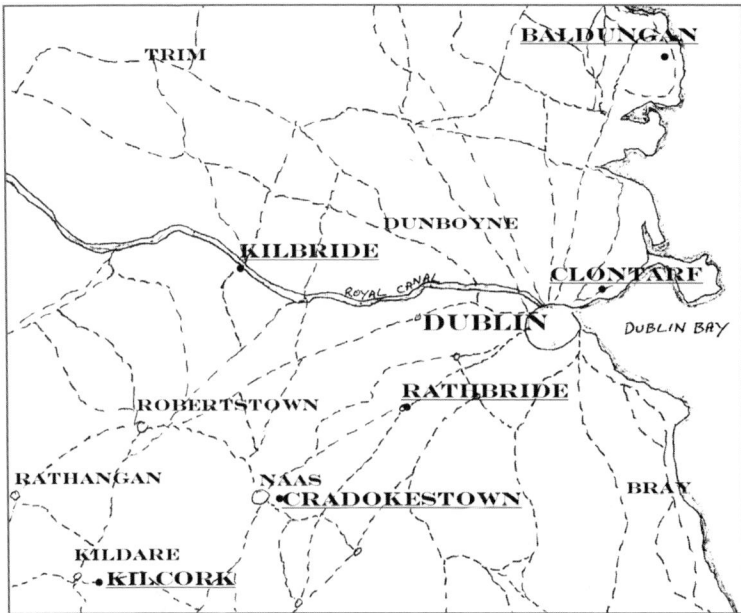

Dublin area, with Templar properties underlined

and paid the king a certain yearly amount as a levy. Some of this land was held by charter by the Templars but no records of this exist today except what is contained in the *Black Book* of Archbishop Alan. This roughly states that William, son of John Lisbone, gave certain lands to the Templars, which included property and the house at Carriglydan and its lands.

DUBLIN CITY

According to the records, there were two Templar tenement buildings or 'frank-houses' situated in the Dublin city of that time. It is noted that after the arrest of the Templars there were arrears of rent on one property that should have been paid by a Henry de Waleton, who seems to have been in possession. The arrears were eventually paid by the Order of nuns of Saint Mary of Hogges who belonged to the Order of Arrouaise.

DUNDRUM

A castle reputed to have been erected by Sr. John de Courcey for the Templars. It remained in Templar hands until 1313 when it was granted to the Prior of Down. After the suppression of all the religious houses in the sixteenth century it was granted to Gerald of Kildare.

GLENMUNDER (Ballyman)

According to the records the Templars held some land and cottages etc. in this locality. They are listed as a castle, four cottages, about 160 acres and some vegetable gardens. The lands were leased out to some of their tenants by the Templars.

KILMAINHAM, Dublin

It has almost always been accepted that the priory at Kilmainham was a preceptory of the Templars. This is mainly due to the false conclusions given in Archdall's *Monasticon* and Archbishop King's MSS and John Gilbert's *History of the Viceroys*. However, in Gilbert's Municipal Documents of Ireland quoting the *White Book* we find a dispute in 1261 between the mayor and citizens of Dublin and the Prior of the Hospitallers at Kilmainham regarding land in that area. The Prior quoted a charter of Henry II in his defence and an inquest held by order of the Justices found that Richard Strongbow had in former times given the Hospitallers and not the Templars the lands of Kilmainham for a foundation.

SAINT ANDREW'S Parish, Dublin

Records show that the Templars had a property here in 1239 and 1308. This was probably a frank (free) house.

TEMPLE BAR, Dublin

There is some controversy as to whether Templebar is called after the Templars or not. During the twelfth and thirteenth century nearly every other Order of monks had property in the ancient city. From the records available to us it is apparent that the Templars had either one or two tenements or 'frank-houses' in the city. On the orders of the Crown the Templar 'frank-houses' were limited to one house in each city, due to certain abuses of not paying tithes. It is doubtful if Templebar got its name from a small Templar house. In fact, the name of Templebar has only existed since the seventeenth century when one of the most prominent merchant families in Dublin, the Temples, had their main abode there.

– COUNTY GALWAY –

GALWAY CITY
According to Lewis, the Templars had a hospital in the ancient town of Galway. There was no evidence of any ruins in his time (1837).

– COUNTY KERRY –

BURNHAM CASTLE, Dingle
According to Smith in his History of Kerry the Knights Templar had a house here and according to Foley (*see Foley. P.178*) the Templars possessed land near Dingle.

This was the seat of the Rice family where a castle was built. Only a few stones indicate the site of the castle. Whether the castle dated from Templar times or later is not known.

DUNGEEL, Killorglin
There are the remains of an old church in this locality and extensive ruins of a castle reputed to have belonged to the Knights Templar. The castle is situated in the centre of the town, on a hill overlooking the bridge over the river Laune. A part of the castle was inhabited up to the 1800s. *Lewis 1835.*

KILLORGLIN

According to Lewis there were ruins of an old church at Dungeel and nearby extensive ruins of the Templar castle which was still inhabited just before his time. This site is east of Killorglin town on the bank of the River Laune. Part of the castle was inhabited up to the 1800s. I don't not know where Lewis got this information but it seems very doubtful that this was a Templar possession. As such there is no mention of it during the arrests and the seizure of the properties of the Templars or during the change-over to the Hospitallers.

– COUNTY KILDARE –

KILDARE

This was a priory and hospital of Saint John The Baptist. It may have been founded by Walter de Riddlesford who was lord of the area, sometime before 1216 for the Cruciferi (Fratres Cruciferi). There is also a tradition that it was built by the Templars. (*see Ware*)

At its height the property included a church, belfry, tower, dormitory, two halls and three other buildings as well as a mill, various cottages and 250 acres of land. Even if there was an early connection with the Templars, Castledermot was, for most of its active existence, in the hands of the Fratres Cruciferi. This order had obscure beginnings in early Christian times in the east. During the crusades they had a hospital at Acre and seem to have had close ties with the Knights Hospitallers of Saint John of Jerusalem. A branch of the order was in England after 1244 where they were known as the 'Crutched Friars'. This name, as well as 'Cruciferi', probably derives from the papal directive of 1245, when Innocent IV ordained that the brethren should carry a cross with them at all times. The Cruciferi were present in Ireland earlier than in England and they had more houses here. *A.310.*

CRADOKESTOWN
There is some confusion as to whether this property was a church or a mansion. Its location was south east of the town of Naas. It was listed as either a house or a church in different sources and connected to the Templars.

GRANEY
A mile or two south-east of Castledermot are the ruins of the Arrosian Augustinian Order nunnery. The convent is said to have been founded by Walter I and the charters were confirmed by Pope Innocent III and by King John in 1207. Close by, there are further remains which are reputed to have been a Templar establishment. These would almost certainly have been associated with the Templar holding at Castledermot.

KILBERRY
Situated about 5 miles north west of Athy, close to the River Barrow on its eastern side, this property has been described as an Abbey consisting of a large ruined church with a tower attached at the north-east, ruins of other stone buildings to the west and a strong fortified tower to the south. The ruins date from Anglo-Norman times and could have been either a Templar or Hospitaller preceptory.

It seems that it very unlikely that this was a priory as all the buildings indicate that it was a defensive castle with a friary. Accepting the tradition that nuns were here, it is possible that there was an adjoining nunnery, in fact a map of County Kildare published in 1902 marks a nunnery in this area. Reban castle is also close by, on the west side of the Barrow.

KILCORK
This property, situated a short distance east of the present Kildare town, was a camera or minor house of the Templars and not a preceptory as first indicated by some sources. This

house was established in the thirteenth century. A castle or a fortified house which was a commandery of the Knights Hospitallers was located nearby and included in the Manor of Tully. The Templar house and property was later handed over to the Knights Hospitallers. *See also Rathbride.*

NAAS
Other Orders, including the Augustinians and Dominicans etc. had churches, houses, hospitals and lands, the Templars only possessed a 'frank-house' in the town. Some sources say that it was a manor house but this is questionable.

RATHBRIDE
Situated two or three miles north east of Kildare town, this is now in the parish of Tully. According to Lewis this was a Templar manor house. He relates that during his visit he saw the remains of a religious house with an adjoining church which was still in use.

Listed as a manor house and lands which passed over to the Hospitallers after the suppression of the Templars but later the lands were exchanged by the Hospitallers to a Thomas FitzJohn, Earl of Kildare for property at Rathmore. The church was retained by the Hospitallers.

– COUNTY KILKENNY –

BALLYLILETHAN (maybe Ballylarkin)
This was listed as a farm or parcel of land but there were ruins of an abbey in the locality. I have no history as such but it was said to belong to the Templars.

GOWRAN (Ballygavern/Ballygowran)
This is situated east of Kilkenny Town towards the border with Carlow.

According to the records the Templars held a small parcel of land here as well as a church. The property's main income was from the church as the holding was very low in valuation. The Templars were engaged in a dispute about the advowson of this church in 1253. We do not know the outcome. In 1710 there was a house in Gowran called 'the Templars' house' (*refer to Athkiltan in Co. Carlow, and to Fotherd, above*). Some sources mention this property as a castle or a fortified house but this seems to be a mistake. In this locality there was also a church founded by Edmund Butler in 1312.

KILKENNY TOWN

According to some records the Templars had some properties in the liberties of the town. It is noted that these properties were mentioned as still belonging to the Templars in 1328 which was after the dissolution of the Order. There seems to be no record of these being taken over by the Hospitallers.

– COUNTY LIMERICK –

AINY

South of Limerick between Bruff and Hospital.
According to Lewis a Templar preceptory was located about five miles west from Ainy. It was founded in 1266 Geoffrey De Marisco.

The name Ainy takes its name from the ancient Irish sun-goddess called Aine who became a fairy queen and a banshee in Irish folklore. The Templar establishment was known as the 'house of Aine' (Ainy). The old ruined church contains a number of interesting tombs. One has the effigies of a mailed knight and his lady while the others have mailed knights in high and low profiles. At the west side of the ruins is part of a tower which is incorporated in the church structure. Not far away are the ruins of a hospital of the Knights Hospitallers.

ASKEATON

Not far from the castle of Askeaton built by William de Burgo was the Templar church with its unusual stone tower. This was said to have been founded c.1270. It was replaced in 1420 by the Earl of Desmond who donated it to the Franciscans (Friars Minor). This was a Templar commandery according to Lewis but Westropp disagreed. The Franciscan friary on this location was built in 1420 and was probably founded by Gerald, the fourth Earl of Desmond. During the Desmond wars the friary was plundered and sacked on a number of occasions.

While under the guardianship of the Crown the church was pilfered and stripped of anything of value by a Roger Cromble who was later arrested but escaped. The castle became the main home of the Geraldines after 1348.

BALLINGARRY

According to tradition, Ballingarry castle was built by the Knights Templar. It is said that the townland – Knightstreet – and the main street of the town derived their names from the Templars. After the suppression of the Order the castle was taken over by the Earl of Desmond's family. A short time later it was taken over by the de Lacys along with other castles in the Bruff area. Some of the de Lacy family were members and associate-brothers of the Templars in the East.

BALLINTUBBER

This very doubtful site is located east of Kileedy and south of Newcastle West. It is mentioned by Lenihan, who ascribes it to the Carmelites while claiming that it had previously been a house of the Templars. It is described as an abbey which was later granted to Robert Brown. This may be a confusion with the Dominican site at Rochestown which was granted to Brown in 1544.

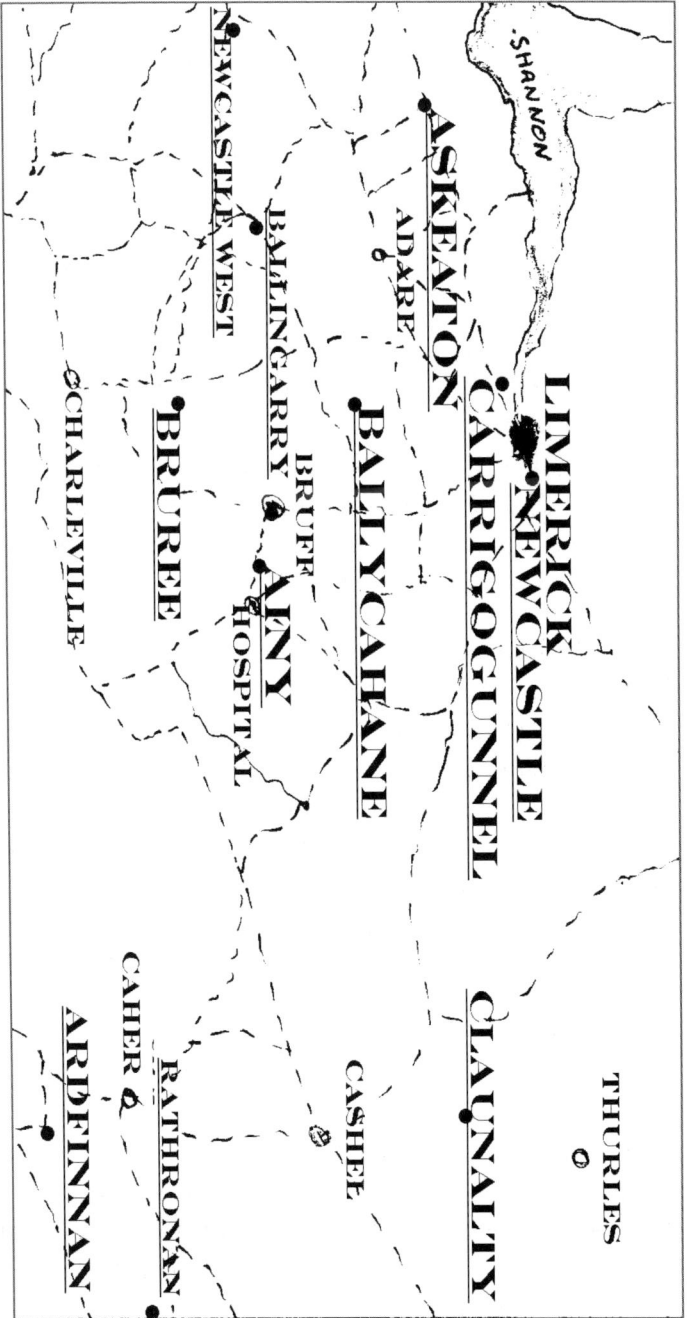

Limerick area with Templar properties underlined

SHANNON

NEWCASTLE WEST

ASKEATON

ADARE

BALLINGARRY

CHARLEVILLE

BRUREE

BRUFF

ANY
HOSPITAL

BALLYCAHANE

CARRIGOGUNNEL

LIMERICK
NEWCASTLE

CLAUNALTY

CASHEL

THURLES

RATHRONAN

CAHER

ARDFINNAN

BALLYCAHANE

A few miles north-east of Croom.

Lewis states that a church dedicated to Saint Cahan was situated not far from Ballycahane castle near Tory Hill. The name of the Templars as well as that of the Hospitallers was associated with this church.

BALLYNOE

There were two castles situated at two different townlands both called Ballynoe and not far from each other. Both of them, according to Westropp and Lewis, were built by the Knights Templar.

One Ballynoe is just south of Bruree. At the location of an old graveyard overlooking the river Maigue was a strong five storey castle close to the medieval church of Saint Munchin. Westrop records a strong local tradition that this castle was originally built by the Knights Templar.

The second Ballynoe is about four miles east of Newcastle West, where the castle is attributed to the Templars by Lewis. It is close to the remains of a seventh century church.

BRUFF

Northwest of the town of Bruff, according to Lewis, is the site of Templebodean (Templeen) which consisted of a church and the ruins of other buildings. It is reputed that Templebodean was founded around 1284 by the Templars.

BRUREE

A castle is said to have been built here by the Templars in the twelfth century. (*Cooke.495. Lewis*)

Lewis stated that a large Templar castle was built here in the 1200s and that they had a church nearby called Temple Colman or Cooleen. These were on de Lacy territory and the lands were probably donated by that family to the Templars.

CARRICK-KITAL, Kilteely

Immediately south-east of Kilteely village there was a castle, all signs of which have long disappeared.

The Templars are reputed to have had a 'house' nearby but according to Lewis absolutely nothing remained of this by the 1830s.

CARRIGOGUNNELL CASTLE

Situated northwest of Mungret near the village of Clarina, this castle is built on a large basaltic rock near the Shannon River. The ruins of the round tower, which is about ten metres in diameter, at the north corner of the earlier heart-shaped bawn and the hexagonal room west of the keep were both attributed to the Templars. Near the east corner are the remains of other earlier buildings. The other additions were built after the suppression of the Templars, who reputedly occupied the castle from c.1210 to 1308. Beneath the ruins are many cellars and passages. (*A.419. quoting MSS Smith*)

Lewis refers to another Templar Castle in this vicinity called Carrig-a-Quincy, which was later granted to the O'Briens. I have no other references but there are various townland names which might suggest a castle site. Carrig west and east and Ballymacashel.

CASTLE MATRIX (Matras)

Situated in the Parish of Rathkeale in the townland of Castlematrix, this site is near to Rathkeale town on the left bank of the river Deel.

The castle is said to have been founded by Gilbert Harvey c. 1289, and in its earlier days consisted of a very strong single tower which measure about 14 metres square, 20 metres high and with walls over two metres thick. It was originally called Castle Matres. In later years c. 1440, when some additions were made to the structure it became one of the principal

Castlematrix as it is today

strongholds of the Geraldine. The Augustinian priory nearby of the canons of Arrouise was supposed to have been founded about the same time. The name Saint Mary's Priory was applied to this religious establishment. However, the term Saint Mary's was usually used for a Templar foundation.

There are two locations in France on the Seine and on the Marne where the Templars had foundations with this name.

CASTLE RAG, Ballingarry

The castle was situated in the townland of Rylaans, near Ballingarry town and according to local tradition, it was a Templar Castle. A short distance away are the ruins of a turret or the bastion of an ancient castle which was once occupied by a branch of the de Lacy family and which is possibly an example of early Templar architecture. Nearby are ruins referred to as the 'Friary', which according to tradition belonged to the Templars. Adjoining this site is the 'Friary field'. Originally the site of a Cistercian abbey founded c.1194 by Donal Mor O'Brien, it later became a Franciscan priory and the walls were still to be seen in 1826.

CASTLEMEINE (Castlemahon Castle)

This is situated a few miles south-east of Newcastle West. This was a strong and imposing tower house of five storeys situated in the townland of Mhoonagh, Castlemeine. Some 300 metres away stood an old church. Nearby stood a circular building with a high conical roof of stone said to have been built by the Templars. This is further reinforced by the fact that the Templars had an establishment close by at Ballynoe. Originally, there were other ecclesiastical buildings in the vicinity. According to Lewis the place was called 'Mayne.'

HOSPITAL

Refer to Ainy above.

KILEEDY (Carrig-a-Quincy Castle)

The castle is situated in the townland of Killeedy North and is about two kilometres east of Glenquin Castle on a minor road north of Ballagh. In ancient times there was a church on at this location, founded in the sixth century and dedicated to Saint Ita.

The castle was reputed to have been founded by King John. The Temple Strand church at Strand which is about a mile north of Glenquin was almost certainly founded by the Templars during the reign of Edward I c. 1291.

KILTEELY

At a site two miles south-west of Pallas Grean on the road to Hospital, the Templars had a church which was referred to as a commandery (*A. 425. Cassells iv.i*). More than likely this was a manor house and not a commandery.

LIMERICK CITY

There was a Templar house situated near the Augustinian friary (*A.232*). This was probably a frank-house (*HW.366*). According to the *Plea Roll No. 13.* - a felon sought sanctuary in a Templar house. Some sources say that there were at least two tenements or frank-houses in the city. No record exists as to the location of the second tenement building.

MUNGRET CASTLE

A few miles west of Limerick, to the north of the main N69 road, stood an ancient castle, said to have been originally a preceptory of the Knights Templar. Parts of the ruins still existed in 1860 but it had vanished from the landscape 30 years later. It was situated about a mile north of the present church where extensive ancient ruins can be found. Following the suppression of the Templars, the manor with its fortified church and small house was transferred to the Order of the Augustinians and later to the bishop of Limerick. According to Lee, the Templars were supposed to have a hospital here.

Its history is connected with nearby Carrigogunnel Castle which the knights were obliged to defend in times of attack. Local farmers related that if the ground was thumped with a sledge in a certain line between the old ruins and the castle

Upper Lotteragh Castle at Bruree, originally built by the Templars

Carrigogunnel Castle

that there was a hollow sound indicating the presence of a tunnel or souterains.

NEWCASTLE (Newcastle West)

This was a fine castle with a round tower and a square tower alongside. Nearby was a church with underground passages which ran down to the river as a means of escape. The castle and church are reputed to have been built by the Templars and the castle later became a seat of the Earls of Desmond.

The church and castle were said to have been built c.1184, some 12 years after King John arrived in Ireland. Tradition relates that when the Templars were accused of heresy and black magic on the instigation of the local bishops and other Orders, the local people rose up against the Templars, killing a number of them while others were burnt at the stake.

OLD KILDIMO

According to *Cassells iii. 431* there was a court castle here built by the Templars near the parish church.

– COUNTY LOUTH –

BALLYBRAGAN (Braganstown)

Braganstown is about two miles west of Castlebelligham. The Knights Templar possessed a substantial holding in this location. During 1284, it was transferred to the ownership of a Nicholas Taffe in exchange for property at Killerger (Killegar) Co. Dublin. When the Prior of Holy Trinity in Dublin claimed the lands of Kilerger from the Templars they received in return two plots at Ballybragan.

COLEY (Coly)

Also referred to as Templetown, this was a Templar manor house and was situated north east of Dundalk near Cooley

County Louth with Templar properties underlined

Point. The lands were previously owned the O'Henrethy who was king of that part of the country. The charter of the endowment is still extant and does not include the establishment of a preceptory or a regular house of the Order. In fact, the details are part of a lawsuit held in Dublin in 1302 between Matilda de Botillere and the Master of the Knights Templar in Ireland, concerning the appointment to the church at Carlingford.

Matilda de Botillere was the widow of John de Botillere and daughter of Matilda de Lacy. In the final summary of the action Matilda de Botillere lost the case.

The property of some 40 acres, the advowson of Carlingford church and the existing tenements or churches at Coley are said to have been originally granted to the Templars by

Matilda de Lacy in 1257. It seems that Matilda was unaware of the number of churches on her estates.

A dwelling house was later built on the property and was described as a small house. At the time of the arrests only a brother Richard, who was possibly a priest, was found to be in occupation. His name was Brother Richard and he could have been a chaplain but more than likely he was a serving brother (*frater serviens*). He was in charge of the farm which had increased from about 40 acres to 240 and included a mill which was probably located in the vicinity of Shillin Hill. Also included were Castle Hazzard and another castle. Like all mills the manorial tenants were obliged in law to use it for the crushing of their crops. Due to its size the brother could not possibly run the farm on his own so he must have had a number of tenants and workers. He also had a brewery where he could make his own spirits. *E.108.*

In the autumn of 1309, Reginald Irp, who was a merchant of Drogheda and one of the provisioners of the king's forces, was authorised to acquire some corn from Coley and Kilsaran. He did not stop there, as he ordered that all the livestock and everything else of value be removed for the king's forces. Whether this action was authorised by the Chancellor of Ireland is another question that remains unanswered.

Afterwards, the manor and lands were first given to Meuerel and Fitz Walter, then to John Kent and later to Walter Dowdall. By this time, it appears that the Crown regarded the Templar lands in Co. Louth as its own property. However, the manor and lands were granted to Richard de Burgo, Red Earl of Ulster, by the Crown in 1310.

It is not known what happened to brother Hugh and Richard of Kilsaran and Cooley as they disappeared from history. More than likely they died in captivity in Dublin Castle. On the twenty-fourth of February, 1314, the manor and lands of the Templars at Kilsaran and Cooley were handed over to the Knights Hospitallers.

CREMARTYN
A church here was part of the Kilsaran manor estate which one of the main preceptories of the Templars in Ireland.

DROGHEDA TOWN
It appears that this property of the Templars was situated between Narrow West Street and the river Boyne and was listed as a tenement building or 'frank-house' which gave the Templars a small return in rent. It was also used as a lodging house for the brethren on their journeys and also for strangers as temporary accommodation. It is not known when this property was acquired by the Templars.

At the time of the arrests it was seized by the Mayor who was accompanied by the Seneschal and a number of bailiffs on behalf of the Crown. The property was handed over to a Nicholas Gerveys and a Robert Coupland. The Hospitallers gained possession after the suppression of the Templars and it remained in their hands until the time of Henry VIII.
See: HW 367.

DROMCATH
This property was listed as a Templar church together with that of Drostreil. The Templars received the income of these churches and their lands. They were probably part of the Templar Kilsaran estate.

KILMADYMOK (Kylmedymok)
Listed as a church which was part of Kilsaran manor.

ROOSKY
All that is left of this Templar property are some medieval remains of buildings which were called the 'priory'. As the

church was pre-Romanesque there must have been another Order involved. The medieval section possibly belonged to the Templars.

– COUNTY MEATH –

GORMANSTOWN
Gormanstown is on the coast just north of Balbriggan. The Templar property here is listed as a church.

Elsewhere in County Meath the Templars had a number of small holdings which were rented out to third parties. These properties included some tenement buildings and were situated in Hawkinstown (Piercetown), Hodgestown and Hilltown.

HILTOUN
Little is known about this Templar property but it seems that it consisted of a house and some lands. Some sources list it as a manor house. Hilltown is about two miles east of Duleek so this is probably the same Hilltown referred to under the entry for Gomanstown, above.

– COUNTY TIPPERARY –

ARDFINNAN
Situated south-west of Clonmel, this was a castle reputed to have been built during the reign of King John c.1184 when he was Earl of Morton and Lord of Ireland. From the ruins remaining in Lewis's time (1837) it seems that it had a rectangular outer wall with square towers at each corner. More than likely there was a substantial tower house within. It belonged to the Knights Templar but was handed over to the Knights Hospitallers after the suppression of the Templars. It later became the property of the Bishop of

Waterford. The church at Ardfinnan had been in the hands of the Hospitallers since 1212.

BALLYSHITHAN
This property was listed as a church but further information was unavailable.

RATHRONAN (Rathernonane/Radraun)
Approximately four miles north-west of Clonmel were a manor house and lands of the Knights Templar.

From the returns in taxes on the property during the reign of Edward III it appears that it was a large property. Sometime after the suppression of the Templars it was taken over by the Hospitallers. During the reign of Queen Elizabeth the master of the Hospitaller's manor at Kilmainham leased out the property to Thomas FitzJohn, the then Earl of Kildare.

TEMPLEMORE
This site is located between Thurles and Roscrea and it is said that the Templars had a castle here but it was destroyed by fire in the eighteenth century. Situated about one-and-a-half miles from the present town, this was probably a minor station for the knights. We have no records of other holdings connected to this castle and a Templar connection to the ancient priory here is not established. Some ruins are still visible at the entrance to the demesne, which consisted of some 200 acres. The church beside the demesne entrance is surrounded by a graveyard within a circular enclosure which is often indicative of an ancient site.
Cassells. iv. 150. Cooke.352.

THURLES
It is said that the Templars had founded a preceptory here as well as occupying the castle. There is also mention of another

castle. All were taken over by the Hospitallers (*Cassells. iv.182. A.675*). However, according to Cooke, the Templars were in possession of another castle in that general area. It seems that this property was handed over to the Hospitallers sometime after the suppression of the Templars.

– COUNTY SLIGO –

EMLYFAD (Emlaghfad) Barony of Corran
This was originally an abbey which was supposed to have been founded by Saint Columcille and is situated about five miles from Ballymote. Near the edge of a nearby lake are the ruins of a Templar House which gives its name to the lake. This preceptory or house was also known as Druimabradh and Teachtemple. Founded during the reign of Henry III, it was eventually handed back to the Knights Hospitallers by Edward II. (*See entry for Temple House in previous chapter*).

– COUNTY WATERFORD –

BALLYVOONY
East of Stradbally, near the coast at Ballyvoyle Head.
Here are the large ruins of a building or buildings said to have belonged to the Templars. *Smith. 73.* On early maps this site is marked as a monastery.

BEWLEY (Beaulieu/Beal)
In the late eighteenth century there were still remains of a monastic building which was traditionally linked with the Templars. These remains had all but disappeared by 1907 although the site has been marked as 'abbey' on Ordinance Survey maps. This was most likely a camera or lesser house and I have no information as to its date of foundation or other history.

KILLURE

Situated south of Waterford on the road to Brownstone Head, this was a preceptory which belonged to the Templars according to various authorities. However, in *Plea Roll 28 Ed.I. m.8.* a Friar Hugh, preceptor of the house of Killeur, was acting as a lawyer for the prior of the Hospital of Saint John. Such an arrangement would not have happened if the prior had been a Templar. Yet, Lewis states that a preceptory was founded here in the twelfth century for the Knights Templar and handed over to the Hospitallers c. 1314. As can be seen from the map of the Waterford area, Killure is situated between Kilbarry and Crooke, both of which were definitely preceptories.

It therefore appears most likely that Killure was always the property of the Hospitallers and that attributions to the Templars are mistakes caused by the proximity of other Templar sites and by the fact that after 1314 Killure and Kilbarry were administered collectively by one preceptor of the Hospitallers. Following the dissolution of the monasteries the property was granted by Queen Elizabeth to Nicholas Aylmer on a lease of 50 years.

RINCREW

This was a castle reputed to have been founded in the twelfth century by Raymond Le Gros for the Knights Templar. (*Cooke. 416*). The property also included a church, kitchen and a refectory.

There is no record of this preceptory being passed on to the Hospitallers but it appears to have come into the hands of Sir Walter Raleigh and the Earl of Cork. In 1541, Rincrew belonged to Molana Abbey, O.S.A. The ruins consisted of a church, kitchen and refectory.

The Templars' 'camera' at Rincrew, Co. Waterford

WATERFORD

In addition to the various sites which have already been discussed and which appear on the map of the Waterford area, I have uncovered some other rather vague references to Waterford.

Henry II granted to the Templars the mills and some marshland between the king's house and the sea.

Included amongst the Templar properties in Waterford was a 'frank-house' in the city and a small island close by.

– COUNTY WEXFORD –

BALLYHOOK (Ballyhack)

This site is on the east side of Waterford Harbour, close to Dunbrody and Kilcloggan. It is also referred to as Balicanock or Ballycaok. Some sources have maintained that this was a preceptory of the Knights Templar who were also in charge of Kilcloggan However, in *Plea Roll 6.Ed.I (m.7.)* Richard de Kalmondesdon, Master of the house at Ballycaok, is joined with the Prior of the Hospital in an action against Philip, son of Benedict.

In addition, Richard is also a witness to a charter of the Prior of the Hospitallers in 1290. It must be noted, that a head of a subsidiary house of the Hospitallers was often called Master while amongst the Templars he would have been called preceptor or brother-in-charge. It seems clear to me that Ballyhook was always a Hospitaller property and that it was later governed by them as an adjunct to the former Templar property of Kilcloggan.

KILBRIDE

These lands are located south-east of Gorey near Courtown. The property at Kilbride was the subject of a protracted dispute between the Abbot of the Cistercian monastery at Dunbrody and the Templars. The disagreement seemed to be centred around the fact that the Cistercians, who were in possession made no attempt to cultivate or build any house on the lands. The Templars withdrew from the dispute when the Cistercians commenced building an Abbey in 1182. The Abbey was also known as the Abbey de Portu Saint Mariae. Originally the lands of Dunbrody were granted to the Cistercians by Herve de Monte Marisco and confirmed by his nephew Strongbow.

After the suppression of the Templars the Crown took over the lands which would indicate that the Templars did have some rights to the property. This is further reinforced by the fact that a John Romayn was accepted into the Templar Order by the Irish Master at Kilbride.

WEXFORD
King Henry II granted to the Templars a church and mills here. The original name of the church was Saint Allochs, which could be the church of Saint Michael, which had adjoining lands.
  CDI.1285/92.

* * *

Taking into consideration the above list and if we accept that about 90 per cent are correct, we are lead to the conclusion that the Templars owned substantial properties in Ireland. It is recorded that they possessed in excess of 30,000 acres of arable land. This figure does not including lands set aside for the grazing of livestock, bog lands, marsh lands, woods or mountainous terrain. A point to be noted is that King Henry III of England ordered that 500 marks be paid from his Treasury in Ireland to the Master of the Templars in England for the construction of a new chapel at New Temple in London. In other words it was the revenue from the Irish Templar possessions that paid for the New Temple chapel.

Arrests of the
Knights Templar in France

On the thirteenth of October 1307, on the orders of King Philip IV, all the Templars found in France were arrested in surprise dawn raids on their houses and castles. They were imprisoned on various trumped-up charges that included heresy, the use of magical powers, irreligious kissing, adoring a cat, active homosexual practices, denying Christ, dishonouring the Mass, perjury and scandals.

This was the culmination of many years work drafting the charges against the Templars by the guileful William de Nogaret, who had previously attempted to arrest Pope Boniface, and ably assisted by Esquiu de Floyran of Beziers and the prior of Montfaucon.

The arrests had been nominally at the request of William Paris, the papal inquisitor in France, in order to avoid the accusation of trespass upon ecclesiastical jurisdiction. Paris, at that time, was the king's confessor and confidant. Jacques de Molay, the Master of the Order, happened to be in France at the time and knew nothing about the arrests until he arrived at the Temple in Paris where he was arrested. He was trying to purchase and organise a fleet of ships to be used against the Muslims in the Eastern Med and for the transport of Crusaders to regain the Holy Land.

Philip IV of France depicted in a woodcarving

The raids on Templar properties were carried out with a certain amount of secrecy in order not to alert the other Templar houses or the friends of the Order. All items of value were removed from the various establishments and transferred to Paris. There is no mention by the early historians or religious sources as to what happened to the riches that had been seized, especially from the Temple in Paris, except that they were used to fill the empty coffers of the Royal Treasury.

The whole operation must have been kept in the strictest secrecy as none of the Templars at court were aware of what was about to happen. There were no whispers or rumours flying around as to the imminent danger to the Order. If the Hospitallers, who occupied the highest positions in court, knew about what was about to happen, they said nothing. Not even a word of warning was whispered, such was the animosity between the two Orders. It should be remembered that the ordinary rank and file of the Templars at that particular time were secular men with little or no education. During the trials the brothers had little or no chance of clearing their names. They were laughed and scoffed at for their lack of knowledge of spiritual matters and of theology. The only option that they had was to confess to the charges and save themselves from burning at the stake. Things were progressing nicely for King Philip.

On the twelfth of August, 1308, the pope issued four bulls in an attempt to counteract the actions of Philip. These are summarised briefly as follows: –

Faciens Misericordiam, in which he appointed commissions in the various countries to examine the Templars. These commissions were to include the diocesan bishop, along with two canons, two Dominicans and two Franciscans for each diocese. Sixteen questions were to be addressed to the Templars regarding their religious practices, beliefs and the accusations against them.

Regnans in Coelis explained the details of the events leading up to the present time and ordered the bishops to appear before him in two years time with their full reports so that he could then decide the fate of the Templars.

Deus ultionum Dominus, in which the pope appoints the prelates as curators and administrators of the Templar goods. This was inoperable in Ireland as the English king had already appointed curators.

Ad omnium fere notitiam, where the pope orders that all the Templar goods that were already seized be returned, under the penalty of excommunication.

Both King Philip and King Edward of England ignored this last directive. After all, they had already seized most of the properties and goods of the Templars and had no intention to return them. When his bishops and prelates reported that none of the seized goods in France, had been returned, the pope wrote to King Philip on this matter. The king's reply on the fourth of December, was that he had done absolutely nothing about the Templar goods, nor would he in future without instructions from the pope himself. This of course, amounted to pure deception on Philip's side. The pope, in a state of despondency, seems to have lost heart as well as his regard for the Templars as the result of such discord and disgrace to the Church. He then issued another bull on the thirtieth of December titled *Calide Serpentis*, wherein he proscribed the Order of the Templars and refused them any papal help or counsel.

In France, the trials were conducted by the Dominican Order in the beginning. Very few witnesses appeared and only written statements were submitted at the inquisitions. It soon became obvious that the charges were fabrications and falsehoods and yet the Templars who had been interrogated, confessed to some charges while others confessed to all after being tortured. In other parts of France, the brothers were likewise tortured before they confessed. A number of sources relate that over 40 brothers died from torture in France.

Imprisoned in small damp cells and existing on bread and water they were constantly woken and brought before their inquisitors. Those that died after torture were secretly buried. It seems that King Philip was unaware of what exactly was happening to the Templars in jail and believed the reports from the inquisitors that the Templars had confessed of their own accord.

News of the arrests and the jailing of the Templars finally arrived before Pope Clement V. The king had acted without his permission and he was furious. He, and only he, had the power to order the arrest of the members of a religious order. This action had superseded his own investigation into the various accusations against the Templars. Nevertheless, he wrote to the other European kings advising them to arrest and interrogate the Templars. This was rather a strange action by the pope as he knew very little about the charges brought against the Templars in France. Neither the king of Aragon or Edward, king of England, believed the charges. James II, the king of Aragon, had previously rejected the charges against the Templars by Floyran when they had been submitted to his court. Fearing an interdiction or excommunication both kings capitulated and the Templars were arrested.

Pope Clement V ordered Philip of France to turn over the Templars to the church authorities. When James de Molay, the Master of the Templars, was told of the pope's decision, he immediately withdrew his so-called confessions and other high-ranking brothers belonging to the Order followed his example. After reviewing the whole situation,

Pope Clement V

Pope Clement V, in February of 1308, suspended all the trials in France after receiving the reports from his church officials.

The matter did not finish there. Philip's answer was to raise popular opinion against the Templars, arguing that it was his duty as their Catholic king to root out heresy in his kingdom. He went to the stage of requesting the opinion of the learned professors at the University of Paris as to whether he had the power to arrest the Templars for heresy. Their reply was that as the Templars were a religious order as such they could not be considered under the king's jurisdiction. However, since all of the Templars were guilty of heresy in the king's own mind, that was sufficient to justify his actions.

In May 1308, Philip and representatives of the bishops, clergy, nobles and advisors from his kingdom went to see the pope at Poitiers to put pressure on him to allow the trials to continue. Fearing for his life, the pope capitulated and agreed, subject to the condition that his bishops supervise the interrogations. And so, the second series of trials began in November 1309.

Jacques de Molay agreed to defend the Order. A man of humble origins, he was without education and lacked knowledge of Latin as well as written French and papal laws. He requested advisors to prepare his defence and that of the Order. He then made another request that he should be heard only by the pope. This condition, of course, was refused. Realising that he did not have the knowledge or training to defend the Order he procured the services of Peter of Bologna, a former procurator of the Order at the papal court who was trained in canon law to take control of the Templar defence.

When the trials resumed in November a papal commission was present to ascertain if the Order was guilty of the charges. Peter of Bologna immediately rebutted the accusations and his defence of the Order was so good that as a warning not to proceed further, 54 brothers were chosen by the king's advisors to burn at the stake on the charge of being relapsed heretics. The effect of this was that those brothers still in jail made no further effort at defending their innocence fearing that they might suffer the same fate.

Early in 1310 over 600 brothers agreed to defend the Order and to state that all confessions were false and given under torture. The reaction of the French inquisitors was swift. They stated that the Templars were now considered as lapsed heretics and on the twelfth of May, 1310, another 54 brothers were burned at the stake in Paris. This was followed by more burnings at the stake in other parts of France. Some brothers managed to escape by paying off their captors while others were murdered in their cells.

The papal commission ended on the twenty-sixth of May, 1311, and the reports were sent to the Council of Vienne, which was to commence on the sixteenth of October with over 300 bishops and prelates in attendance. Ireland was represented by the archbishop of Cashel and the bishops of Emly, Killaloe and Cloyne. The majority of those attending agreed that there was insufficient evidence before them to condemn the Templars. It was the intention of all those present to hear properly the accusations that were brought against the Templars without undue interference from any quarter, especially the French Crown. When word reached Philip that the results of the Synod were going against him, he realised that his future plans were in jeopardy

Templars burning at the stake from a medieval chronicle

and immediately set out for Vienne in February 1312 with his army. It was his intention to influence the pope and to urge him to dissolve the Order of the Templars even if it involved giving their goods and properties to another Order of knights.

When the king's army surrounded the Synod the pope capitulated, and by his bull of the twenty-second of March. *Vox Clamantis*, dissolved the Order of The Templar and by a further bull of the second of May, *Ad Providam*, he entrusted the Knights of the Hospital with all the goods of the Templars and ordered his bishops and prelates to carry out these decrees in France, England and Ireland.

King Philip convinced the pope to appoint three Cardinals and his friend, the archbishop of Sens, to carry out the decrees in France. It is recorded that a group of Templars who were still free appeared at the Council to defend the Order but quickly vanished!

A parliament was called by King Philip, to be held in Lyons in March, 1312. After a brief discussion Philip marched with his army to meet the pope in Vienne on the twentieth. Two days later, the pope issued a papal bull, *Vox in Excelso*, in which he stated that the Templars had not been found guilty of any of the charges brought against them but that the name of the Order had been defamed. With the king breathing down his neck, he was left with no option but to dissolve the Order. The delegates to the Council were furious that a proper ecclesiastical enquiry was not heard but no debate on the matter was allowed by the pope.

Those Templars who had been declared innocent or who had confessed and been reconciled with the Church would receive a pension and were given permission to live in the former houses of the Order. As for the brothers who had not confessed and had been judged guilty of heresy, they would have to go through another trial. Amongst these were four of the senior brothers of the Order: Jacques de Molay, Geoffred de Charney, Geoffred de Gonneville and Hugh Pairad, Jacques de Molay and Geoffred de Charney were condemned to die at the stake while the other two were to be imprisoned for life.

It was obvious from the trials and the activities of the crown that Philip IV wanted to get the Templars convicted by any means possible. Four years had now passed since the first arrests and he was again desperate for more money. He wanted to soak every bit of income from the Templar properties. He became so engrossed in his quest for money that he even threatened anyone that disagreed with his financial policies would be accused of heresy and also burned at the stake. In fact, Philip felt himself under threat from all the kingdoms around him including the pope. It is said, that he had a mad idea to personally lead a new crusade which would finally liberate the Holy Land and that he would form a new military Order for this end. Of course, a new crusade was out of the question with all of Europe in a state of unrest and uncertainty. In addition, a serious change in the climate caused the failure of crops resulting in a famine.

It was on the second of May, 1312, that Pope Clement V announced the dissolution of the Order of the Templar in his bull, *Ad Providum*, giving all the Templar possessions to the Knights of Saint John which was mentioned earlier. The only exceptions were the Templar castles in Spain. The Hospitallers, in turn, were to compensate Philip IV for his expenses in arresting, jailing and interrogating the Templars. Neither Philip nor the Council of Vienne was happy with this papal directive as everyone had their eyes on gaining the properties of the Templars.

Now it was the turn of the Hospitallers to find themselves accused of evil deeds, vices and fraud, and of spending their wealth on themselves and on their magnificent 'palaces.' Realising that they could not change the decision of the pope, the council issued a number of further conditions, i.e. that all the Hospitallers privileges should be suspended and that all able bodied knights should be sent to the Holy Land. They were also to arrange that their properties be looked after by a few brothers and that all parishes and churches were to be handed over to the local bishops. Only when these conditions were fulfilled could the Hospitallers receive the lands of the Templars.

The Hospitallers were now getting a taste of what the Templars had been through. However, with the deaths of Philip and of Clement IV in 1314 nothing was done about reforming the Hospitallers.

The next pope, John XXII, began to put the finances of the Hospitallers in order and endeavoured to ensure that all the Templar properties, with the exception of those in Spain, be handed over to the Hospitallers. When they moved in, they removed anything of value that still remained, in case the king or the original donors could claim possession. All the relics and items of value that still remained were moved to the Hospital in Malta in 1130, where they remained until that island was taken over by Napoleon in 1798 on his voyage to Egypt. The Hospitallers were evicted from Malta and the relics and treasure were either looted by the French soldiers or were moved out secretly from the other side of the island to some unknown destination. It is said that only God knows where they are now!

Before moving on, it is interesting to note that many elements of the persecution of the Knights Templar were not unique to their case. In 1238, Pope Gregory IX, had accused the Hospitallers of heresy and ordered them to correct their ways. In addition, with his decree *Ad Nostrum*, he outlawed the beliefs of certain lay groups of men and women who had religious houses.

In 1252, Pope Innocent IV licensed the use of torture in cases dealing with heresy. It should be recalled that the traditional punishment since Biblical times for religious dissent was death by burning. Later, in the fourteenth century, Pope John XXII, condemned the Spiritual Franciscans as he believed that they were prone to religious excesses and were against the rules of ecclesiastical authority. About this time, the Teutonic Knights, who were still in existence, in Livornia were accused of heresy by their political enemies. An enquiry was ordered by the pope but no evidence was found to substantiate the claim.

See Appendix, The Chinon Code, which presents new evidence regarding the last days of the Templars in France and their belated direct contact with the pope.

ARREST OF TEMPLARS IN ENGLAND

Hugh de Payens, the first Grand Master of the Templars visited England in 1128. He had already met the king in Normandy, France, who had given him money and gold. His visit to England was to meet the barons and to recruit crusading knights for the newly established Order. Many gave him gifts of silver, gold and donations of lands. This bequeathal of lands was granted on the condition that the Templars would pray for the souls of the donors and their families. Very few donations were given towards the Templars' activities in the Holy Land.

With the donation of lands increasing during the following decades the earliest group of Templars to arrive followed the example of the Cistercians in how they administered their own houses and lands by the use of lay brothers. In a short period of time, the number of Templar properties increased dramatically, rising to over 34 establishments around the countryside. These properties consisted mostly of low-lying marshland or heavily wooded areas that required reclaiming and clearance. The Templar properties were known as baileys. Their preceptories, generally, had living quarters, a church and a cemetery. There was only one Templar hospital established, which was situated in Lincolnshire.

When the position of the English Master was created, he resided at the preceptory at London, which was called the Temple of London and later became known as the Old Temple. This base was established in 1144, following the many grants of lands made to the Templars by King Stephen c. 1135. The Old Temple was in the parish of Saint Andrew, north of Chancery Lane. The Templars moved to a new property known as the New Temple in 1161. This became the main treasury of the Crown and a safe place where the barons and knights could keep their valuables. Amongst the relics kept at the New Temple were two crosses, which contained pieces of wood from the True Cross.

King Edward I used the Templars' northern preceptories for the storing of food, livestock and supplies during his Scottish Wars. On one occasion, he stayed at Temple Cowton on his way to Scotland in 1300. His son, Edward II, was king for only four months when the Templars were arrested in France on the orders of King Philip IV who was Edward's future father-in-law. When a copy of the charges against the Templars was sent to him, he refused to believe them but he knew he had to tread gently.

Pope Clement also found himself in an almost similar situation when Philip threatened that he would reopen the case against the deceased Pope Boniface, whom he accused of heresy and sodomy, which would bring down the papacy. Edward was reluctant to arrest the Templars despite the threats of Philip IV but when the pope issued a papal bull, *Pastoralis Praeemientitiae*, requesting that all Templars be arrested, he was obliged to follow the papal instructions, fearing that the pope would place an interdict on his kingdom and possible excommunication for himself.

Being in possession of a copy of the 104 charges against the Templars in France, he requested his bishops and members of the other Orders within his kingdom to make their own list. They came up with a total of 54 charges, which were based on reception into the Order, heresy, idolatry, sodomy, lack of charity and using false pretences to obtain properties. He began to worry when he observed the charge of sodomy on the list. Most historical commentators agree that Edward himself was a homosexual, so it is no wonder

Edward II of England

that he thought that he himself might also be charged with sodomy if matters got out of hand.

Nevertheless, he instructed that orders be sent to all county sheriffs on the fifteenth of December, 1307, that they were to gather 24 trustworthy and honest men and be prepared to receive further instructions on the following Sunday. As arranged, the sealed documents were distributed to the sheriffs on the appointed day. They had to swear an oath of secrecy before the contents were revealed. The instructions were that all Templars should be arrested and all of their properties seized. These orders were not to be carried out until the ninth and tenth of January, when every sheriff in the country had received the following instructions:

'On Wednesday next after the Feast of the Epiphany in the morning the brethren of the order of the Temple, are to take an inventory of their goods and muniments in the presence of the keeper of the place, to wit a brother. The sheriff is then to cause their bodies to be safely guarded elsewhere than in their own places, but not to place them in a hard or vile prison, and to find them sustenance. The sheriff is to certify to the treasurer and the

barons of the exchequer when he has done this, and to send the names of the brothers arrested and of their lands.'

The Templars probably expected their arrests, knowing what had happened in France and of the arrival of the pope's bull at the royal court. Some no doubt fled into temporary hiding either in England or in the far north of Scotland. It is recorded, that most of the Templars were still at large in 1310, when further orders were issued for their arrest.

William of La More, the English Master, was arrested on the ninth of January and imprisoned at Canterbury. The numbers arrested were only about 153 and most of these were old men, along with a few young members who had recently joined the Order. Neither group had seen service in the Holy Land. Most of the preceptors were allowed to remain in their preceptories until summoned to appear before the Inquisitors. Those of the knightly Order were located in the New Temple, while the others were mostly sergeant-brothers and chaplains who were in the main preceptories. Nothing is mentioned about associated-brethren.

Following the inventories, the lands and preceptories were administered by trustworthy men who were appointed by royal court or by the sheriffs themselves. Many of those who were nominated to take care of the lands were favourite barons who were close to the king.

When the inventory of all the Templar establishments was completed, little of value had been found. It became obvious that the Templars in England were living in poverty and true to their vow. Only the barest necessities of life were found. Very few arms were encountered in the searches, only a few bows, swords and bits of armour. There was no sign of the 'famous' Templar treasures, not even in the New Temple, except for those items which were held in safe-keeping for the king himself and the barons, knights and rich people.

The papal inquisitors arrived in England on the thirteenth of September, 1309. They were the Abbot of Lagny and Sicard de Vaur and a notary. They were joined by the archbishops of Canterbury and York and the Bishops of Chester, Durham, Lincoln and London. The French Abbot expected that confessions would already have been made, but this was not the case, since torture of clerics was not allowed under English law.

The Inquisition was held in the Priory of the Holy Trinity in London. No confessions to the charges were forthcoming and the Inquisitors requested permission from King Edward to use torture. This was not granted but the Templars were placed in chains in the cells of the Tower of London. By this time, Edward had received instructions from the pope that the Templars should be tortured so that confessions might be made. Edward passed over the responsibility of the Templars to ecclesiastical authorities thus ridding himself of any responsibility for the trials which continued during the following years.

The inquisition was considered a failure. Very few of the Templars admitted guilt. Most of the Order were sent to other monasteries to pray and do penance.

Arrests in Spain, Portugal, Northern Europe and Scotland

At this stage, it is interesting to see what happened in the Christian kingdoms of Aragon, Castile, Leon and Barcelona in Spain and other countries such as Portugal, Germany and Bohemia.

Spain

After the First Crusade, the pope saw that the fight against the Moors in Spain was the same as a Crusade and exhorted the knights from every country to go to Spain to fight the infidels. Pope Paschal II (1099-1118) even went to the stage of banning Spanish knights from going to the Holy Land.

As the Moors were gradually pushed south, the Templars arrived in Spain and were appointed protectors and grantees of lands previously held by the Muslims. Alfonso I of Aragon preferred to appoint Templars to these roles instead of his barons whom he did not trust. By this time, he had already organised groups of knights, like the Order of Santiago in the kingdom of Leon, to fight against the Moors.

These Orders were similar to the Templars and followed the Rules of the Cistercians, but married men were allowed to join and to sleep with their wives. They enjoyed the best of both worlds as long as they succeeded in staying alive.

Templars' castle of Almourol, Portugal

The Templars tried to retain their Moorish tenants by offering them special privileges but most moved south to the Moorish kingdom. Being low in numbers, the Templars had no alternative but to rent out some of their properties. In addition to parcels of land the Templars were given a number of castles and fortresses by the noble families which were strategically placed to defend the kingdom from French or Moorish invasions. When the Templars were requested to open a new front against the Moors, they at first refused but later capitulated.

In the royal court of Aragon, the Templars became advisors to the king. They mediated between the king and his nobles as well as representing him in Rome and loaning money to the monarch, the nobles and the merchants at a low rate of interest. When the necessity arose, the king was in a position to summon them in his fight against the French or the Saracens.

Being without an heir, king Alfonso, made a will before his death, whereby his kingdom was left to the Canons of the Holy Sepulchre, the Templars and the Hospitallers as he expected that there would be a war amongst his barons over succession. This arrangement was not accepted by the Spanish barons and instead the different Orders were granted parts of the kingdom which they were obliged to rule and defend. In this arrangement the Templars got control of a number of castles and a fifth of all lands recovered from the Moors outside the kingdom.

During the succeeding years the various kings of Aragon requested the Templars to assist them in their struggle against the Castilians and the French. They were reluctant to accept the directive but, being under the threat of losing their lands and privileges, they agreed as Aragon and Spain were probably the most important areas where the Templars were established in Western Europe. It was one of the main sources of funds, recruits and materials for the struggle in the Holy Land. With the demand for funds and loans from the various kings and the costs involved in equipping recruits and maintaining supplies for the Holy Land the Templars found themselves under constant pressure financially.

The Templar influence at the royal court of Aragon began to decline as they became more and more involved in dispatching recruits, money, horses and equipment to their brothers in the Holy Land. However, when war broke out between Charles of Anjou and the king of Aragon over the kingdom of Sicily, the Templars took the side of the king of Aragon while Pope Martin IV, who happened to be related to Charles, took the side of his relation and diverted into the conflict part of the new Crusading army destined for the Holy Land. He also provided money to Philip III of France who had gone to the assistance of Charles of Anjou. To justify his actions, the pope declared that this campaign was a 'Crusade' against the king of Aragon.

King Alfonso X, king of Castile and Leon, also had Templars in his court. Yet, he preferred to have locally founded military Orders to defend his kingdom. These were the Order of Calatrava and the Order of San Julian de Pereiro which were both founded in the 1170s. When the pope put forward the idea that all military Orders should be joined together in one unit, the major objections lodged were from the kings of Aragon, Castile and Leon in Spain.

It was the middle of October, 1307, when King James of Aragon received a letter from Philip IV of France listing the charges against the Templars. Philip advised James to arrest all the Templars and to seize their properties. King James refused to believe the charges and sent back a letter to that effect. He also sent letters to the same effect to the other kings in the various European countries. He refused to believe the accusations made against the Templars by de Floyran and other conspirators. Sometime earlier, de Floyran, an ex-Templar who had been thrown out of the Order, had made the same submissions to the court of King James.

Pope Clement V requested King James to take steps to arrest the Templars and informed the king that he and he alone had the right to dispose the Templar properties in France and in Aragon, Castile and Portugal. Reluctantly, King James ordered the arrest of the Templars and the confiscation of all their properties. A number of the Templars were arrested and properties were seized. However, some of the Templars retired to their castles and decided to hold out against the king's forces.

Still believing that the Templars were innocent of the charges brought against them, King James could not let their substantial holdings fall into the hands of the pope. He even offered tracts of land in his kingdom and in the rest of Spain to two nephews of the pope in exchange for the major tracts of Templar lands and their castles. This proposal was rejected by the pope. In the circumstances, King James had no other alternative put to seize the Templar properties and ordered his army to lay siege to the Templar castles hoping that they would be starved out. After some months the important castle of Miravet surrendered and the other castles followed.

An Inquisition into the so-called crimes of the Templars followed. No confessions were forthcoming as torture was forbidden in Aragon. Many of the noble families beseeched the king to release the Templars as they had family members amongst their ranks. Those Templars that had been arrested were allotted good living conditions with adequate food and wine. In March, 1311, the pope ordered the archbishop of Tarragona and the bishop of Valencia to use torture on the Templars to elicit confessions. However, no confessions were made. The same action was taken in Castile, Leon and Portugal without results. Meanwhile, King James demanded from the pope that all the castles and fortresses should remain in his hands as they were vital for the protection of his kingdom against the French and the Muslims. These negotiations went on for years.

To replace the Templars the King brought a new military Order into existence with a base near Valencia. This new Order was to under the guidance of the Cistercians.

Eventually, the Hospitallers got possession of most Templar properties as the ex-Templars either joined monasteries, left the clerical life and got married or became mercenaries.

In the kingdom of Castile the king seized most of the properties of the Templars but some of the noble families who had donated land and castles to the Templars took possession of these. The pope was not happy with these actions and ordered that all the properties be transferred to the Hospitallers. This argument went on for years.

Meanwhile, in Portugal, King Diniz took possession of all of the properties of the Templars and founded a new military Order to replace them. This new Order called the 'Order of Christ' was later given the Templar lands.

Germany and Northern Europe

In Northern Europe, despite the fact that no damning case could be brought against the Templars, their properties were seized. The barons, who were mostly sympathetic to the Templars took possession of most of the properties in Germany and Bohemia while the Hospitallers eventually got the remainder. As a repayment for running the inquisition against the Templars, the Dominicans got possession of the Templar houses at Vienna, Strasburg, Esslingen and Worms.

In northeastern Europe the situation was quite different. The Templars did not move into this region until after the turn of the thirteenth century. They were introduced as protectors to the Cistercians, Dominicans and Franciscans who were engaged in the conversion of the pagans on the eastern borders.

By then, the Teutonic Knights had already well established themselves in this region. But these were not the only military Order, as the Order of the Knights of Christ and the Order of Christ of Dobrin already existed. These latter two Orders were later integrated into the Teutonic Order of Knights. In spite of the presence of the other Orders, the Templars received many donations of lands where they built fortresses or castles.

With the other Orders the Templars were engaged in the struggle against the Mongols on the eastern borders, which was not so much a religious struggle but a war over territory. During the Mongol invasion the Templars lost many brothers and fighting men. Their castles were captured and much of their influence disappeared while the Teutonic Order became the main military Order in that vast region of many small kingdoms which were always in conflict.

There was no uniformity in the way in which the Templars were arrested in the various countries and kingdoms. While some were arrested, the majority fled or disappeared. With their lands and houses confiscated they had no other alternative but to join the Order of Teutonic Knights or integrate themselves into secular life.

Arrest of the Templars in Scotland

The activities of the Templars in Scotland were largely hidden from history until the record of deeds and records of their foundations were found by chance at Faxfeet and Temple

Cowton. Scotland had its own Master who was under the authority of the English Master. The Order was invited to Scotland by King David I in 1128 and Hugh de Payens made a visit. He was granted some land at Balantrodoch where a preceptory was founded later. In fact, no lands were registered to the Templars before 1185. Later, other grants of lands were made by the important families in the south of Scotland and the main possessions and preceptories were located at Balantrodoch (Temple), Maryculter, Swanston, Temple (Kirk Liston) and Gullane. The principal preceptory was at Balantrodoch which was also known as Temple.

In 1291 the Order was brought into serious disrepute by the new Scottish Master (1286-1292) known as Brian de Jay. Along with the Master of the Hospitallers, he had sworn fealty to King Edward I at Edinburgh Castle. This action was against the Rule of the Order. He fought during the Scottish wars on the side of Edward I and was killed at the Battle of Falkirk in 1298. It is recorded that nearly all Templar and Hospitaller properties were destroyed during the Scottish Wars. The pope of the day excommunicated Edward Bruce and placed an Interdict on Scotland.

The lands at Culter (Maryculter) were granted to the Templars by William the Lion of Scotland but the preceptory was not built until some time later. When more land was donated around Culter by William Bisset this preceptory had in excess of 8,000 acres of land and a church was built by the Templars for their tenants. It is interesting to note that no Scottish family names appear on lists of Templars residing in Scotland.

With Scotland under a papal interdict and Edward the Bruce excommunicated since 1306, it is possible that Templars from both Ireland and England took refuge in that country where papal or ecclesiastical power did not exist.

The arrests of the Templars by the agents of the English Crown quickly followed those in England. Only two Templars were apprehended, namely, Walter Clifton, preceptor of Balantrodch, and William Middleton, preceptor of Culter. It is not known to where the other brothers disappeared. More than likely small numbers took flight into the wilderness of North Scotland. The inquisition was held before the Bishop of Saint Andrews and the Papal Nuncio, John de Solerio. Despite the fact that over 50 members of other Orders, as well as William Saint Clair and his brother gave evidence, they were acquitted and absolved of any crimes. However, they ended up at the Cistercian monasteries to do penance and repent.

Much has been written regarding the Saint Clairs and Roslin (Rosslyn) Chapel but there is no documentary evidence connecting the Saint Clairs and the Templars. The unsubstantiated supposition that the Templars in Scotland came back into society as the Freemasons, will be examined later as will the purported appearance of Templar and Hospitaller knights at the Battle of Bannockburn.

Arrests of the Templars in Ireland

The French Templars were taken completely by surprise when arrested. In England and later in Ireland, the Templars must have expected their own arrests as they would have learned from their own sources about the papal bull sent to King Edward. From the records of that time it is clear that only two Templars were arrested in Scotland, fifteen (some sources say 30) in Ireland and 153 in England. It is interesting to note that out of the combined number only 15 were knights with the remainder either sergeants or chaplains. Of those questioned in Dublin most had seen over 40 years service with the Order. This might also explain from the details of the inquisitions in the various countries that the majority of those questioned were of advanced age indicating perhaps that there were very few recruits to the Order during its latter years.

Edward II and his council, were loathe to execute the orders of the pope but still followed the example of Philip IV of France, and ordained that all possessions of the Templars, throughout his dominions, should be seized. The Writ for the arrest of all Templars issued by the king of England was sent to John Wogan, the Crown Justiciar and Treasurer for Ireland. Copies were forwarded also to the English officials in Ireland for their own guidance. They were instructed to arrange a day for the execution of their instructions without delay. This had to done before reports arrived in Ireland of the events in France and in England where the document had already been circulated. From a point of interest the Writ is quoted herewith:

'*For certain reasons it is ordained by the lord, the King, and his Council, that on Wednesday next, after the feast of the Epiphany next coming, that all the brethren of the Knighthood of the Temple in every county of England (and Ireland) be attached by their bodies by the sheriffs thereof, and by some lawful men of the same counties; and that all their lands, tenements, goods, and chattels, as well ecclesiastical as temporal, be seized and taken into the hands of the said King, together with the charters, writings and muniments (titles to lands) of all kinds belonging to the said brethren, and that of those goods and chattels and of the value thereof be made a lawful inventory and indenture (in the presence of the keeper of every of the places of the said brethren, whoever he be, a brother, namely, of that Order or another person, and in the presence of two lawful men neighbouring and nearest to the said place who can conveniently be present), one part whereof shall remain with the said keeper and the other with the sheriff, under the seal of him who shall have caused those goods and chattels to be so seized, and that those good and chattels be placed in safe and secure custody and that the cattle and beasts of the said brethren be well kept and maintained.*'

The Writ then goes on to say that the Templars should be kept safely, securely, and faithfully, in a suitable place, elsewhere than in their own dwellings, so that their keepers may be sure that the brethren shall receive reasonable sustenance as becoming their rank paid out of the things and goods that are seized. In addition, the sheriffs should send a letter to the Treasurer and the Barons, letting them know

Medieval illustration showing the burning of Templars

how many had been arrested, their names, and to where they have been sent to custody. Also, the sheriffs should let it be known what lands, tenements and goods had been seized.

The method of alerting the sheriffs in Ireland was probably the same as in England. Firstly, writs were sent to the sheriff to advise him to recruit ten or twelve lawful men of their counties. Then the king sent out the sworn clerks with the writ against the Templars and their properties etc. which were to be delivered to the sheriff on the understanding that all were sworn to secrecy until the writ had been executed.

This order was to be executed without fail. On the morning of the feast day the order was carried out and the Templars were arrested and transported to prison. It was reputed that Gearoid, fourth son of Maurice, Lord of Kerry, being Grand Master of the Order in Ireland at that time was also imprisoned. There is only one source which mentions this and there are doubts about its actual veracity.

The Templars in Ireland were not dealt with harshly. After all, their co-brothers of the Hospital had fought for the English Crown. William FitzRoger, the Commander of Kilmainham, with many of his brothers, had been captured in 1274 by the Irish at Glendelory (Glenmalure) where many were put to the sword. Later, in the years 1296 and 1301, William's successor, William de Rosse was Lord Deputy of Ireland and in 1302 was appointed Chief Justice of Ireland.

On the twenty-ninth of September 1309, further orders came from England that all those Templars who had not already been apprehended were to be arrested and transferred to Dublin Castle jail, which might indicate that there were some of them still at large having avoided arrest. It is more likely that some had fled to other houses belonging to the Order, which were situated in remote parts of Ireland where English rule was almost non-existent, such as Dingle, Galway and Sligo. From these ports they could embark on vessels to other safe countries.

As was the case in England, some of the Templars were committed to monasteries to do penance while the inquisition continued. The king also granted them their own manors of Kilcloghan, Crooke and Kilbarry where they could stay. They were allocated four pence per day as an allowance. The Grant Master received two shillings. To their chaplains was given three pence per day and 20 shillings per year for the care of their horses. Servants were allowed one penny per day.

Almost all sources give the number of Templars arrested in Ireland as 15 but a few give the number as 30. However, in actual fact the exact number was 18. Due to the speed of arrests the majority of the Templars that were apprehended were located at the main preceptories, such as Clontarf, Co. Dublin, Colley and Kilsaran in Co. Louth.

Those Templars that were arrested in the first sweep were:

Henry Tanet, the Irish Master of the Templars
Henry of Aslackby
Richard de Bistleham
Ralph de Bradley of the Preceptory of Crook
Hugh de Broughton
William de Chesby
John de Faversham
Henry de la Forde, Jr.
William Kilross
Adam de Langford
Peter de Malvern of the Preceptory of Kilcloghan
Henry Montravers
Thomas le Plamer of the Manor of Kilbarry
Robert de Pourbriggs
Robert of Romayne of the Manor of Rathronan
Richard de Upleden
William de Waryne of Clonaul Manor
Thomas le Palmer

A number of the above did not appear at the trials. It is presumed that they died in prison at Dublin Castle as the majority were of advanced age, or else they could have bribed the gaolers to arrange their escape. Amongst these were Ralph de Bradley, Peter de Malvern, Thomas le Palmer, Robert of Rathronan and William de Waryne (Marne).

The Writ and the instructions did not reach the Irish Justiciar until the twenty-fifth of January, 1308. Despite the short notice, the Justiciar quickly organised everything and on the third of February the lands of the Templars were seized and the knights were escorted to Dublin Castle while a complete inventory of each preceptory and house was executed. These inventories can be located in the certificate of the Barons of the Exchequer sent to England (I Edward III). According to all the inventories the goods on the Templar estates were valued at £716.16s. 6d, which amounted to very little in those days considering the great wealth that the Templars were supposed to possess.

The precise details of each inventory down to every fork and knife indicate that the inventories were thoroughly carried out and the absence of anything of value raises many questions. There were very few books, and only a small number of lances, swords, helmets, a bow and body armour were located and the amount of coinage found amounted to about £10. There is no mention of horses, bridles or saddles or quivers of arrows. There is also no mention of deeds or manuscripts located but later some of these turned up in 1312 during disputes over the ownership of some of the Templars' properties. According to the instructions of the king and his council all details of the inventories should have been forwarded to the English exchequer but this did not happen until years later.

What followed next was the appointment of guardians and stewards to each of the important properties who were obliged to collect the usual rents and services from the tenants. At the time of the arrests rents were due and now the collectors were instructed that all monies owed should be paid forthwith. It can be gathered from this additional instruction that the king was short of money as the conflict with the Scots was proving expensive. He also made demands on the Irish Treasury for money and supplies for his troops.

On the nineteenth of June, 1308, the king instructed his Justiciar and Treasurer in Ireland that in addition to the supplies already requested he should send 1000 quarts of wheat, 1000 quarts of oats, 200 quarters of beans and peas, 300 tons of wine, 3 tons of honey, 200 quarts of salt, and 1000 stock (salted) fish. These were to be paid for from of the proceeds of the sale of Templar goods if this was sufficient, otherwise the English Treasury was to be debited for the amount outstanding even though everyone knew that the Treasury had no funds.

When the arrest of the Templars was carried out and the inventories of all their houses were taken, it became clear that the members of the Order lived a very frugal life and demonstrated that they had very few earthly possessions or comforts. As some of the preceptories and houses were vacant for a period of time, a certain amount of looting took place and it is assumed anything of value was removed. An example would be the removal of the grinding stones from the mill at Clontarf.

If the number of preceptories and houses is compared with the number of Templars arrested it is obvious that not all of them were apprehended and only those who were either serving-brothers or preceptors were imprisoned. It is probable that some had fled the country when word reached them of the arrests in France and England. As regards money, the most likely place would have been the preceptory at Clontarf where the income from all the Templar possessions would have been stored before transfer to the Temple in London.

According to the records of the English Inquest of 1185 and the Inventories of 1308, the value of the Templar properties had increased by over 50 per cent and the rents had doubled as had the number of tenants. The income from the holding of markets and fairs had also increased substantially.

An inventory of the goods and chattels seized from the Templars after their arrest is preserved in the Public

Record Office, London (class number E 101/239/11.) This was possibly sent from Dublin to the English Exchequer around Easter 1326, which was some 16 years after the event. It was requested in December 1325 under mandate by the bishop of Lincoln and treasurer of England. Due to its deficiencies and omissions the treasurer and barons of Ireland were reprimanded. The inventories mentioned give a detailed breakdown of all the foundations of the Templars and what animals, goods and chattels were listed during the various seizures. Although, the lists are extensive in some instances giving details down to spoon and knife they do not mention anything of value which is rather unusual in the circumstances.

It is interesting to note that all the coinage collected from all the houses on the inventories was but a small amount. It should be mentioned here that the brothers were not allowed to carry any money on their person except when they travelled to make some purchase or other. All change had to be handed back to the preceptor who kept all monies in a strong box in his room. What happened to these strongboxes is another unanswered question! Also, the arrests followed the end of the harvest season which would indicate that all rents, dues, and the income from the sale of crops etc. would have been in the possession of the preceptor before being transferred to London.

There are no records that diocesan enquiries were held in Ireland but papal inquisitors did arrive to oversee the provincial enquiries in each country. It was the king and not the pope who had advised the bailiffs and trustworthy men in Ireland, in relation to the seizure of the assets of the Templars. Among those who made up the commission into the Templars and their assets in Ireland, on behalf of the pope, were Thomas de Chaddesworth, Dean of Dublin,

Clontarf Castle

Bindus de Bandmellis, Canon of Saint Paul's, diocese of Florence, and John Balla, Canon of Clonfert. They were also instructed to assist the inquisitors sent by the pope to England. In addition, he ordered the archbishop of Dublin to be present in England when the inquisitors held their meetings. The king finally ordered John Wogan, the Justiciar, to take steps that all Templars still at large should be arrested and sent to Dublin Castle. There are no records showing that any Templars were rounded up during this later action. It is quite possible that any Templar still free had fled the country by sea either to Scotland or to Portugal where they would find some degree of safety.

TRIALS OF THE TEMPLARS IN IRELAND

The Templars who were imprisoned had to wait nearly two years before they were tried as the inquisitors didn't arrive in Ireland until September 1309. The actual trials did not commence until January 1310. During this delay one of the Templar Masters called Henry Tanet was transferred under guard to London where he was accused of making treaties with the Saracens. This indicates that he was one of the few Templars in Ireland who had seen service in the Middle East.

Some fourteen Templars gave evidence at Saint Patrick's Cathedral in Dublin. Most of them were older men with over 30 years service to the Order. They all denied the charges set forth against them. Many hostile witnesses gave evidence before the court including members of the other Orders. Due to a lack of evidence of the charges made against them the court was adjourned and the Templars were released on condition that they stayed in the named preceptories i.e. Crooke, Kilbarry and Kilcloghan, where they could do penance and repent their sins for the remainder of their mortal existence.

Seeing the Templars in their robes being marched or taken by open carriage to Dublin and back to their preceptories no doubt caused excitement and public attention. This must have been the main topic of conversation. It is difficult to image what the people's thoughts were at that time. Unfortunately, on the subject of records, the Templars wrote very little about themselves in Ireland or elsewhere and the only thing that exists today are copies of letters mostly sent from the Holy Land describing the situation and requesting money.

The inquisitors that were sent over to Ireland to arrange the enquiry were listed and the proceedings were recorded. These records can be found at the Bodleian Library at Oxford. The inquisitors were Richard Balybyn, Philip de Slane and Hugh Saint Leger of the Dominicans, Roger de Heton and Walter Prendergast of the Franciscans. These were joined, on and off, by John de Mareschal, Canon of Kildare, Philip de Hendelee of the Dublin Archdeaconry, Matthew de Welland and Philip de Wylabi of the church at Ballygriffin, Dublin.

Hugh Tanet, the then Master of the Irish Templars on his return from England, was the first to be questioned, followed by Richard de Bistelesham, Ralph de Bradley, John de Faversham, Henry de Forde, Henry de Hasellakeby, Adam de Langeport, Henry Mautravers, Robert de Pourbriggs, John Ramayn, Richard de Upladen and a chaplain called William de Kilros. All of these were interrogated three or four times. They were accused of the following: of denying Christ at their reception into the Order; of being told by those receiving them that Christ was not the true God and did not suffer for our redemption; that the preceptor made them spit on the Cross or offer it some other mark of indignity; that they did not believe in the sacraments of the altar; that the priest of the Order did not use the proper words by which the body of Christ is made at the canon of the Mass; that the grand master or preceptor could absolve them from all sin; that they made and adored idols; that at reception they received and indulged in unclean kissing; that they were forbidden under oath from revealing certain practices; that they were ordered to confess to the brotherhood of the Order who could absolve them; and that the brethren swore to advance the interests of the Order by any means possible above anything else.

It is interesting to note that amongst the witnesses for the prosecution only four lay people, including an ex-servant of the Order gave evidence. The remainder were all clergy and included brothers Roger de Heton, Hugh de Lummour, Walter de Prendergast, Nicolas de Kilmay and Walter Wasphayl of the Franciscan Order; Simon de Dachemound, Richard Kissok, Gilber de Sutton, Richard de Balybyn, Thomas de Racho, Nicholas Bakun, Richard de Boclonde, John de Balmadoun, Robert de Lusk, Lucas Chyn, Thomas Cadel also of the same Order. The rest were from other Orders and included Thomas, Abbot of Saint Thomas the Martyr, Simon, Prior, and Marestellus; Richard de Gromekyn, Ralph Kilmaynan, William le Botiller, Henry of Pembroke, Henry de Stone, Gilbert de Rene, John Gay, Philip de Kenefeke, Roger, all of the Order of Saint Augustine; Henry de Wallens, David Longus, John de Waterford, Hugh le Marescall, John le Palmer and John de Serde also Augustinians.

From the beginning of the Inquisition in Dublin it was obvious that the majority of the witnesses had nothing to offer except rumours and gossip. Roger de Heton and Hugh de Lummour said that they believed the charges because the Templars had already confessed them to the pope. This was completely incorrect at that time. Another, called Walter de Prendergast, accused the Templars of scandalizing the Church. The Abbot of Saint Thomas the Martyr in Dublin accused the Templars of denying Christ. There was no evidence or witnesses to these charges. Others stated that the brethren did not look at the Host when the Eucharist was celebrated but looked down at the floor. The inquiry lasted from the end of January to the sixth of June without anything damning being offered in evidence. As a result, the Templars were absolved, ordered to do penance and were escorted to their houses where they were to pray and repent their sins.

It is impossible to say if torture was applied to the prisoners as it was in France and later in England. The fear of the rack and torture was sufficient in both those countries to obtain a confession. It is recorded that two of the Order died from torture in England. The pope postponed the Synod of Vienne until October, 1311, as the enquiries into the Templars were incomplete. About this time the Grand Preceptor of England, Scotland and Ireland died in prison refusing to confess to heretical doctrines. The results of the enquiry in Ireland are not known except that no Templar was found guilt as charged.

It has already been stated that some of those who had been imprisoned at Dublin Castle, like murderers and felons, had been allowed to return under house arrest to Kilcloghan, Crook, Clonaul and Kilbarry where the produce of the manors would sustain their existence. Following the papal bulls, those still in jail in the Castle were probably released to the provincial Synods.

From the time of the seizure of the Templars' lands in 1308 they had been mostly managed by the agents of the Crown. The agents also received tithes, and income of the various churches. They also appointed bailiffs where necessary, employed servants and collected the rents. A certain amount of what was collected was paid to the Irish Exchequer by the agents/commissioners. No doubt there was a certain amount of fiddling with the records of returns as supervision of these was almost non-existent.

On the second of May, 1312, the pope wrote to the archbishops of Armagh, Dublin, Tuam and Cashel and others to defend and assist the Knights Hospitallers who had been placed in possession of the Templar lands in their respective diocese. Yet, the Hospitallers were forbidden to enter their newly acquired properties by order of the king (first of August 1312) or to meddle in the goods and lands of the Templars until after his next Parliament. During the next six months King Edward continued to let out the Templar properties in Ireland to the friends of the Crown. As an example, on the twelfth of May, the king allowed Nicholas de Balscote, Baron of the Exchequer to hold the lands at Kilcloghan and the church of Ballygavern at a yearly rent.

With little or no progress in acquiring the Templar properties in Ireland, the Hospitallers were getting more than anxious about the transfer. On the twenty-fifth of November, 1313, Brother Albert de Nigro Castro, preceptor of the Hospital of Jerusalem and Leonard de Tybertis, Prior of the Venetians and the procurator-general of the Hospital sent a petition to the king to hand over goods and lands belonging to the Templars. The king could not ignore this petition and immediately ordered the guardians of the Templar lands in England and Ireland, which included the Justiciars, chancellor and treasurer in Dublin, to hand over to the Hospitallers the lands and goods that had previously belonged to the Templars. As the excuse for this action the king stated that he had to conform to the pope's recent bull. However, he made sure that his and his subject's interests were to be preserved, which was a nice way of saying that he intended to hold onto some of the properties.

Following this instruction, the Prior of the Hospitallers in Ireland was ordered, on the twelfth of February 1314, to continue to pay the Templars their allowance of two pence per day for their sustenance. The following month the king issued his writ ordering Nicholas de Balscote to hand over the Templar lands in Wexford which he held, to Roger Utlawe, Proctor of the Hospital, Walter del Ewe, Prior of the Hospital and to Brother William de Ross. An interesting point in this writ is that the king mentioned that above all the 'ornaments of the churches' are to he handed over. This could have meant the church plate and anything of silver or gold used for the celebrations of the sacraments. To say the least, this seems a rather senseless order as most of these items had probably being seized in earlier years or had already been sold.

According to the records, some of the Templars in England were assigned monasteries where they were to complete their penance. The two pence per day allowance for the Templars was either not paid or was found to be insufficient or the Hospitallers declined to pay the amount. Even though the Order had been dissolved since March of 1312 and the goods and property had been assigned to the Hospitallers, we find the pope, on the first of December, 1318, ordering the deans of York, London, Canterbury and Dublin, as well as the Priors of the Friars Preachers and the Friars Minors, to examine the stipends made by the various archbishops in the kingdom and bring the amount up to a level necessary for the support of the ex-Templars. The pope also informed the above that all sentences issued by the archbishops and prelates against the Master and brothers of the Templars were to be revoked. This was rather an unusual order as it contradicted the bull *Vox Clamantis* issued in march 1312.

Notwithstanding the various papal bulls and royal writs, the Hospitallers encountered great difficulty entering the Templar lands and properties in both England and Ireland which had been assigned to them by the pope. The feudal lords were more than reluctant to allow the lands granted by their ancestors to pass to anyone but themselves. To sort out this matter a conference was held in 1324 which the king, his prelates, nobles, barons and other important men of the realm attended. Despite objections, the king and his nobles agreed that 'as the Order of the Templars was instituted for the defence of Christians against its enemies that their lands and houses should be delivered to other holy and religious men of the church', namely the Knights of Saint John of Jerusalem.

It is evident that this Act did not have the desired effect as in 1329 we find the pope still writing to the king of England, exhorting him to make restitution to the Hospitallers of the property of the Templars. In Ireland, it seems that the Hospitallers gained access to most of the Templar lands. This was verified by the inventory made at the time of the dissolution of the Monasteries.

Templar Myths and Legends

The question of whether the Templars were guilty of their 'crimes' or not has been debated down through the centuries since the suppression of the Order. One would have expected that the Templars' trials and subsequent downfall would have been the end of the Order, and that it would have vanished into obscurity but this was not the case.

From the fourteenth century onwards, many authors debated whether the Templars were guilty of the charges or not. One of the most damning propositions was put forward by the German, Henry Agrippa, in his book *De Occulta Philosophia,* which was published in the sixteenth century. In it he claimed that the Templars were depraved, corrupt and used magic for their own ends. Other commentators soon followed, stating that the Templars were guilty of witchcraft and magic.

Writers during the following centuries took different sides in a period when the occult and magic pervaded everyone's minds. It is no wonder, therefore, that the Templars made an appearance in the Holy Grail stories, particularly those by Wolfram von Eschenback, where the Templars were portrayed as guardians of the Holy Grail. From this time onwards, other stories appeared which accepted as factual the idea that the Templars were the rightful guardians of the Holy Grail, which they had hidden in some safe place where it could not be found. There was however little agreement as to what the 'Grail' actually was. In contrast, Sir Walter Scott, who was a fervent Protestant, in his *Ivanhoe* and other stories from the Waverley Novels portrayed the Templars as dishonest, corrupt and cruel. These writings gave a bad image to the memory of the Templars.

The eighteenth century saw the rise of many secret societies. A Scottish writer by the name of Andrew Ramsey propounded the theory that there was a link between the Templars and the Freemasons. He argued that both the Templars and the secret society of the Freemasons had Scottish origins and that the Masons were descended from the Crusaders, namely, the Templars, due to the connections of both groups with the Temple of Solomon. This was further 'verified' by the Templars having been called the 'Knights of the Temple of Solomon' and the Masonic rites and rituals being based on the building of the Temple. This erroneous supposition was soon accepted as fact by the educated middle class, and numerous groups of Freemasons came into existence, each claiming a direct connection to the Templars.

At about the same time, a new Masonic society appeared in Germany claiming that its rituals were derived from the Templars through Jacques de Molay. This Masonic lodge also claimed that the Templars had secret wisdom and the power of magic which had been handed down to them. Not to be outdone, a group of Frenchmen 'discovered' the Larmenius Charter which stated that Jacques de Molay had named John Larmenius as his successor as Grand Master of the Templars before he was burned at the stake. Despite the fact that the document was a very poor forgery its contents were accepted as fact by the French Masonic Lodge. They believed that they possessed a tradition going back to the Templars which justified their existence and that the claims of all other Masonic lodges were false. This was the beginning of the period when all Masonic lodges vied for their own respectability and credibility especially in Scotland, Germany and France.

During the latter half of the eighteenth and the beginning of the nineteenth centuries many Freemasons conveniently discovered 'documents' or 'evidence' that their ancestors were connected to the Templars. Included amongst these was a group who were members of a Scottish lodge and claimed that they were descended from Templars who had sought refuge in Scotland at the time of the suppression of the Order in England. These Templars were originally supposed to have joined the Masonic craft guilds. The claims did not stop there. A John Robinson asserted that a number of Templars had evaded arrest in England and went underground and had established a secret society.

One of the most unusual claims, which was made by a section of the Freemasons that originated in Scotland, connected the Sinclair family, Rosslyn chapel and the Templars. According to their 'ancient tradition' Hugh de Payens, one of the founders of the Templars, was married to Katherine Saint Clair, of the French branch of the family. However, it is well-documented that Hugh de Payens founded the Templar Order after the death of his wife whose name is not mentioned in any records. This questionable link was to justify the Sinclairs who became the Grand Masters of the Scottish Freemasons.

This connection seems rather strange as there are no records confirming any connection between the Templars and the Sinclairs. The records do, however, reveal that two of the Sinclairs, William and Henry, gave evidence against the only two Templar preceptors that were arrested in Scotland. This questionable relationship was manifested by the building of the famous Roslin (Rosslyn) Chapel by Sir William Saint Clair in 1446 which commenced over a hundred years after the dissolution of the Templar Order. From the available records it seems clear that there were very few Templars in Scotland at the time of the suppression of the Order and it is extremely unlikely that there were still a number of them living there a hundred years later or that a Sinclair was nominated as the Grand Master.

No expense was spared in the building of Rosslyn Chapel, which was a mixture of gothic, French and other foreign architectural influences. Every surface of the interior was covered in carving and decorations. Built as a collegiate chapel it was supposed to be a place where monks could continuously offer prayers for the souls of the Sinclair family. According to some novelists, it was the place where the Holy Grail was hidden in a secret room under the sacristy.

The connection between the Templars and the Freemasons really came to the fore during the late seventeenth century. In order to give these secret organisations a proper basis in history and a lineage, the members based their institutions on secret rituals which they connected with the Temple of Solomon in Jerusalem. Each organisation or Lodge had their own rules and ceremonies with each striving to validate their own particular existence

In the early nineteenth century a German writer, called Joseph von Hammer, was one of the first people of more modern times to connect the Holy Grail and the Templars. Following the theories of Wolfram von Eschenbach, he began to influence educated people by stating that the Templars were the guardians of the Holy Grail. Traditionally, the Grail was thought to be the chalice used by Christ at the

Rosslyn Chapel, Scotland

Last Supper and was supposed to be the key to eternal life. In all the stories about the Grail, the Templars are portrayed as knights who are holy and of royal birth. These knights are not bound by the vows of poverty, chastity and obedience but have dedicated their lives to God. The legendary connection between the Templars and the Grail became the basis of many other secret societies who claimed that they possessed esoteric knowledge and were versed in the use of magic.

There were various theories as to the whereabouts of the Holy Grail. One was that it was brought to England by Joseph of Arimathea and hidden in a Templar preceptory. Another was that it was taken to Scotland by a number of Templars when they were avoiding arrest and was eventually hidden in Rosslyn Chapel. Also, there is the claim that the Holy Grail was buried on the Hill of Tara. This resulted in the arrival of many Freemasons in Ireland who commenced to dig up parts of the ancient site.

Combined with the myths of the Templars and the Grail is the symbol of a red cross on a white shield which was part of a knight's armament. The red cross on the white shield was the symbol of martyrdom during the Middle Ages. In comparison with this theme the shields of the Templars had a turtle dove. This was the symbol of eternal love.

Mention must also be made of Chartres Cathedral which was supposed to have been built by the Templars according to the French architect Louis Carpentier. It was reputed to have been the location where the Holy Grail was hidden and was also a repository for ancient wisdom.

Another legend concerns the Sword of Destiny which was also known as the Lance of Longinus. This was supposed to have been the spear of the Roman centurion which pierced the side of Jesus on the cross and was also used to place the vinegar filled sponge to His lips. Both the spear and the

Exterior of the Temple church in London

sponge were offered to the pope by the Ottoman leader called Beyazit during the fifteenth century. According to the legend associated with the lance it is said 'that whoever possesses the Holy Lance and understand the powers it serves, holds in his hand the destiny of the world for good or for evil'. It is reputed that Adolf Hitler believed in this power and removed the lance from the Vienne museum when he took over Austria.

Another version of the same story, which has Welsh origins, states that Joseph of Arimathea brought the Holy Grail and the Lance to England and deposited them at Glastonbury.

They eventually ended up in the hands of King Arthur and the knights of the Round Table.

As for the history of the 'True Cross' there are many stories. According to certain sources Helena, mother of Constantine, Emperor of Rome, made a pilgrimage to the Holy Land, in her old age. During the demolition of the various temples on the Holy Mound, ordered by her son to make way for new churches, a piece of wood was discovered bearing the inscription 'Jesus of Nazareth, King of the Jews.' This piece of wood, whether it was a forgery or not, was accepted by Helena and the Christians in Jerusalem as a relic of the 'True Cross'. It was then encased in a gold cross and placed in the new church of the Holy Sepulchre.

In 614 when the Persians captured Jerusalem the relic was taken as a trophy to Persia. Many centuries later it was said to have been located during the siege of Constantinople by the Templars and brought back to the church of the Holy Sepulchre in Jerusalem. However, no records exist that the Templars were involved in the siege of Constantinople.

During the final stages of the Battle of Hattin it appeared again, held aloft by the Bishop of Acre before he was struck down. According to some sources it was removed by some of Saladin's men. Others claim that it was taken by a Templar and hidden in the sand; however, when he returned some time later he was unable to locate the relic. It next appears on the Dome of the Rock before Jerusalem was taken by Saladin who ordered its removal. It was then dragged through the streets by men on horseback for two days and nights.

The relic made a reappearance at Acre in July 1191 when that city fell to the forces of Richard the Lionhearted. Later, it turned up at the conclusion of the siege of Damietta when the Christian forces were about to withdraw. Al-Kamil, brother of Saladin, agreed to hand back the relic as a sign of peace but it could not be located. Where it went after that, nobody knows. There were numerous reports – too many to mention – of the possible location of the relic including the Paris Temple. There are some vague references that there were two crosses which contained relics of the True Cross in the London Temple.

Another tale to surface during past years was that the 'head' that the Templars were supposed to have worshipped was 'the head of God'. This theory was contradicted by Joseph von Hammer in his book *The Mystery of Baphomet Revealed* in which he stated that the 'Templar head' was a Gnostic idol called Baphomet. He did not seem to know that the Gnostics never worshipped idols and that Baphomet was an old French word for Mohammad. Despite his many erroneous assumptions, the teaching of Joseph von Hammer received wide acclaim in Germany.

In later years, even up to the twentieth century, many theories surfaced as to the origin and meaning of the 'Templar head'. One theory put forward claimed that it was the head of John the Baptist. Another stated that it was the embalmed head of 'God made Man', which the Templars had located in the Temple of Solomon after many years of searching. Some even came to the conclusion that the 'head' was in actual fact the Holy Grail.

In recent times, another theory postulated that it was a copy of the head on the Turin Shroud, which was to be found in the cathedral of Turin and which many Catholics believed to be the shroud of Christ. Some people said that the 'Templar Head' was the actual shroud itself. This theory claims that the shroud was that of Jesus Christ, and was supposed to have been located by the Templars at the siege of Constantinople and which they guarded with their lives. However, modern analysis has dated the shroud to the period

1320-1340, which was after the dissolution of the Templar Order. No doubt, there will be many more theories surfacing about the 'Templar head' during the coming years, such as the idea that the shroud is that of the dead Jacques de Molay before his body was burnt at the stake.

When the Templars' properties were seized and inventories made, nothing of great value was found in spite of the many rumours of their vast wealth. During the centuries that followed the dissolution of the Order, many theories and reports surfaced as to where the Templar treasures were hidden including one claiming that a local priest at Rennes le Chateau in France near the Pyrenees had discovered buried treasure not far from the location of a ruined Templar preceptory. Where exactly the treasure was found and what happened to it seemed to have quickly vanished from circulation. A number of writers adopted the claim as the basis of further stories concerning the Templars. This was followed by the claim that the Templar treasure was buried on the Danish island of Borneholm.

In connection with the disappearance of some of the Templars and their supposed treasures, an Irish Franciscan monk named Simon encountered an ex-Templar, by the name of Peter, in Egypt during 1323. He had married and was one of a number of knights who still protected pilgrims journeying to the Holy Land from Egypt. They still practiced their faith but had abandoned the Rules of the Templars. As mentioned in *Hybernia Ad Terram Santam*, these knights were extremely wealthy and possessed much gold, silver and precious stones. They also wore expensive garments of silk and lived in luxury in Cairo.

Another account comes from a German chaplain named Ludolf of Sudheim, who encountered two ex-Templars, who had earlier been imprisoned by the Muslims, during his pilgrimage to the Holy Land. He gives no further details as to what conditions they were living in.

Yet another far-fetched tale told of a Templar fleet which, after the arrests of the members in France, sailed from La Rochelle to North America, landing first at Newfoundland where they buried their treasure.

Among those who became very interested in the Masonic movement was the English Admiral, William Sydney Smith, who made attempts to expand the movement during his voyages overseas. Another was a James Burnes, c. 1840, who outlined the modern ideals of the Masonic Lodges as poverty, avoidance of evil and obedience to the Grand Master. The rituals of the Lodges were a modern version of those supposedly enacted by the medieval knights and were based on structures which had no real historical basis.

Many books written about the Templars could be classified as 'fictional history' based on legends and myths. Others like Umberto Eco's *Foucault's Pendulum*; *The Last Templar* by Michael Jeck; *The Knights of the Cross* by Piers Paul Read; *Set in Darkness* and *The Falls* by Ian Rankin; and the *Da Vinci Code* by Dan Brown, however thorough or far-ranging their historical research, do not purport to be anything but fiction. Other writers, like Robinson, or Baigent and Leigh in their best seller *The Holy Blood and the Holy Grail*, have put various theories about the connection between the Freemasons and the Templars into public circulation, including the story that Jesus did not actually die on the cross but married Mary Magdalen and settled in the south of France.

It might seem surprising that no fictional story has yet been written about the activities of the Knights Templar in Ireland, especially with the existence of a legend that the prophet Josephus brought the Ark of the Covenant to Ireland after he fled Egypt.

APPENDIX

The Chinon Code

Further details of the arrest and the trial of the Templars in France have been revealed in the document known as the Chinon Chart or Code. This Code is made up of documents written by the papal scribes when the papacy was based at Avignon, France between 1309 and 1378 CE. These documents were later transferred to the labyrinth of the Vatican secret archives where they remained undisturbed for many centuries. It is only recently that the cipher formulae of the Papal Chancery were decoded and the contents of some of the 349 books were revealed.

In the document known as the Avignonese 48, part of the trial of the Templars including the only enquiry held by Pope Clement V himself, at Poitiers in the summer of 1308, is revealed. The proceeding of this enquiry is contained in the original form (*mundum*) and in a summary (*Rubrice*) which also contained many private annotations. In fact, these annotations contained a wealth of further information which could be deemed to be of more value than the original documents.

In view of all the damaging rumours that were in general circulation regarding the Templars Pope Clement decided to undertake a formal investigation (*super statu Templi*) into the Order and he communicated this decision to King Philip of

France in early August 1307. This pontifical investigation was about to commence in October when news arrived that the Templars had already been charged with heresy and jailed the previous day. In Paris, Guillaume de Nogaret, as the keeper of the Royal Seals, announced before a large gathering at the palace that the Templars had been found guilty of heresy.

Following the arrest and capture of the Templars under the orders of King Philip the Fair and their subsequent confessions under torture, the Pope was never allowed to interview the Knights during the initial part of their trials (October 1307–June 1308) as they were now regarded as self-confessed heretics. However, Clement was finally able to personally question and judge the Templars at a special inquisition held at the papal court at Poitiers without the influence of King Philip and his legal teams.

Acting on a decree of King Philip issued on the fourteenth of September 1307, his soldiers broke into all the Templar preceptories on the thirteenth of October. This whole action was unlawful but the king to give it some respectability appointed Guillaume of Nogaret to be the Keeper of the Seals replacing the Lord of Belleperche who was friendly with the Templars. The Franciscan brother Guillaume de Paris, who had been the formal prosecutor during the French Inquisition, was also recruited. The confessions of the Templars under torture were recorded by royal notaries and immediately dispatched to the Pope as proof of heresy.

Guillaume de Nogaret and Guillaume de Paris were both intent on the downfall of the Templars for different reasons. As a Franciscan monk, Guillaume de Paris, envied the status bestowed on the Templars by successive popes. Guillaume de Nogaret, on the other hand, had a deep hatred for both the papacy and the Templars which originated during the Albigensian Crusade or the suppression of the Cathars in southern France.

It appears that Guillaume could never forgive Pope Innocent or any successor Pope for the deaths of his relations, who were Cathars, and the destruction of his homeland by 'foreigners' from the north of France. Such was the depth of feeling in this conflict that the loyalty of the Military Orders was divided between the pope, the Christian kings of France and Aragon and the renegade Count of Toulouse. The Templars were present if not participants in the massacres of Marmande and at the castle of Monsegur where both Cathars and Christians were put to the sword or burned as heretics.

During the fight against Catharism, Pope Honorius III granted the Inquisitor in Tuscia, northern Italy, some extraordinary powers to suppress heresy. These powers extended even to all the Orders including the Hospitallers and the Templars. These powers were never revoked and were used by French royal lawyers against the Templars in a legal action by the Crown which took the whole matter out of its religious context and ultimately out of the hands of the pope. As a result of this action Pope Clement found himself in a serious quandary and a solution was sought during the papal consistory of the 16–18th of October. Either he could excommunicate Philip, which would result in a schism, or else take a more temperate line. He eventually issued a papal bull *Ad preclaras sapientie* in which he rebuked the king's actions against the Templars but still gave Philip a way out of the dilemma. When the papal bull was delivered to the royal court by the papal notary, Geoffroi de Plessey, a forgery was immediately written wherein it was stated that the pope had entrusted the king with whatever actions he had taken against the Templars. This was not the first time that the lawyers of the royal court had produced a forgery of a papal bull.

Unaware of this situation, Clement sent Berenger Fredol and Etienne de Suisy to Paris to collect the Templar prisoners and bring them back to Poitiers. They were not permitted to see the Templars or to remove them from jail. Faced with the resignation of his ten most important cardinals and the collapse of the Curia, Clement sent Berenger Fredol, his nephew and Etienne de Suisy again to Paris in December 1307 as if the first visit never took place.

On this occasion they were not just papal legates but were given the power to excommunicate King Philip and place the kingdom of France under an interdict by the pope if the Templars were not handed over. This had the desired effect and Philip wrote to the pope on the twenty-fourth of December advising him that he would deliver the Templars and promised that he would keep separate the affairs of the Templars in his administration. Yet, Philip delayed as much as he could and the transfer of the Templars into the hands of the pope's representatives did not take place until some time later.

In February, the pope suspended Guillaume de Paris and the entire team of the French Inquisition. Immediately, libelous letters against the pope were circulated trying to influence him in recommencing the trials but the Pope would not comply. As a result, Philip tried to distance himself from the charge of torturing Jacques de Molay. Yet, the slander and pressure continued against the pope mainly orchestrated by Guillaume de Plaisians, Nogaret and Pierre Dubois. Even when his family was threatened the pope would not change his mind. Finally, in June 1308, Philip agreed to hand over the Templars to the pope's representatives.

Seventy-two Templars, mostly those who had confessed or were just servant members, were dispatched from Paris to Poitiers chained together in open wagons and under an escort of the king's troops. Also included were Jacques de Molay and three other high officials of the Temple.

When the wagons of prisoners finally arrived at the royal castle of Chinon not far from Poitiers, Jacques de Molay and the other three officials were detained in the dungeon of the castle. Philip excused this action by saying that the prisoners were too ill to complete the journey to Poitiers, but this was far from the truth and just a ploy to complicate matters further since no papal inquisition could be complete without the leaders of the Templars. He was also afraid that the pope might grant absolution to Jacques de Molay and his jailed companions.

The papal hearing referred to as the '*inquesta in Romana Curia facto Templariorum*' was held in Poitiers. Those papal dignitaries who presided were Berenger Fredol (the pope's nephew), Etienne de Suisy, Pierre de La Chapelle-Taillefer, Thomas Jorz (England), and the Italians Landolfo Brancacci of Naples and Pietro Colonna. The hearing commenced on the twenty-eighth of June and continued until the first of July in the presence of a consistory of Cardinals mostly chosen by the pope but which still included a number who had been made cardinals by the previous popes including Cardinal Pietro Colonna who was friendly with King Philip and who had previously been excommunicated by Boniface VIII.

On the second of July, the pope held a public consistory and gave his plenary absolution to the Templars who had confessed to their misdeeds or heretical views and who had gravely asked forgiveness of the Church. This type of absolution did not indicate acceptance that the Templars were completely innocent or that they were guilty but was a solution for the pope in the circumstances. In the back of his mind, Clement knew that they were not heretics, but some of the accusations against them had some basis in fact and he wished to get to the bottom of the matter when he interviewed them himself.

Under cross-examination they admitted that during their entrance ceremony they had denied Christ and spat on the Cross when they were threatened with prison or death and that they, as soon as possible, confessed this to a priest and asked for absolution.

Clement, in this regard, believed that the statements of the Brothers interviewed were so contradictory that they could be accused of heresy but might be guilty of blasphemy.

The pope was left in a quandary and decided that the matter needed further examination.

From the annotations made on the margins of the register Avignonese 48 (mentioned above) the views of the papal supporters became known as regards the Templar's guilt.

The findings were confusing to say the least. Even the pope, before the Council of Vienne held in 1811, shut himself away in his rooms to try and analyse the confessions.

It is not known if the side notes detailing the above facts were written at the hearings in 1308 (original parchments) or from other documents or a bunch of notes (minutae) made at the oral hearings of the Templars which were taken down in a type of shorthand by the papal notaries. From the marginal notes and the original sources of the Templar confessions it is possible to understand the views of both the pope and the inquisitors on the entrance procedure of new recruits to the Order which was actually in force for over a hundred years.

After the formal admittance ceremony a type of secret addition or appendix was followed whereby the new recruit had to experience what he might have to suffer if he was captured by the Saracens, i.e. he would be compelled to deny Christ and to spit on the Cross. By enduring this type of initiation the faith of the new recruit would be fortified for what may lay ahead. In addition, he had to endure another test to prove his obedience and respect for his seniors by kissing his preceptor on the lower spine, on the navel and finally on the mouth. The relations and general public who attended the main ceremony of initiation did not witness the latter additions. As these procedures were so revolting and abhorrent, Jacques de Molay instructed the main preceptors of the Order to uproot the practice before it could seriously affect the Order. But the damage had been done – Nogaret and his aids were already well aware of the practice which had been confessed during the torture of the Templars.

Whether these practices had been brought to the attention of the pope before the arrest and imprisonment of the Templars is debatable. However, in the report of his heated meeting with Jacques de Molay in the spring of 1307 these secret rituals were discussed. After the pope's discussions with the Templars at Poitiers he knew that he could not condemn them for heresy as their actions during the secret rituals were only pretence. At most, the only charge that could be brought against them was apostasy which was a sin that could be forgiven and he therefore absolved those that were brought before him at Poitiers.

What happened in the case of Jacques de Molay and the other Templar leaders that were held in Chinon castle, is another question. The pope could not absolve them if they were not in his presence. Yet, according to the register of Pierre d'Etampes, the king's Chancellor, a letter was written to Philip by three cardinals advising him that Jacques de Molay and his companions at Chinon had been absolved of all sin 'in the name of the pope' in the summer of 1308.(*see: Vitae Paparum vol.3. 98-100 by Baluze*)

No other reference to the above existed until Barbara Frale found some interesting material in the Vatican Archives in 2001. Located amongst the list of provincial enquiries ordered was a parchment detailing one headed by three cardinals which had the formal seals of Berenger Fredol, Etienne de Suisy and Landolfo Brancacci who had been appointed by the pope to hear and to judge the Templars held at Chinon. It stated that Jacques de Molay and his companions were absolved by the papal deputies and ordered that they should receive the sacraments once again. This was known as the *'inquesta in diocesi Turonensi'* which corresponded with the register of Pierre d'Teampes. The Chinon chart has, therefore, explained the events surrounding the captivity of Jacques de Molay and his companions at Chinon Castle but has also left a lot of unanswered questions.

Amongst the details it seems fairly clear that Guillaume de Plaisians and Guillaume de Nogaret and the royal gaoler, Jean de Jamville were present at Chinon castle where they were given a letter, which was to be delivered to King Philip by the three cardinals, outlining the fact that Jacques de Molay and his companions had received absolution and had been accepted back into the Church. Even though they were present at the castle, the two royal lawyers were unaware that a hearing had been conducted by the three cardinals without them being present. This was a coup for the pope and his cardinals as Philip had done everything to prevent the pope or his cardinals meeting Jacques de Molay. The pope advised King Philip in his bull *Faciens misericordiam* that the Grand Master of the Templars and other high officials had been absolved and reconciled with the Church and that nobody could ever examine or judge them again, this power being reserved to the pope alone.

The funny thing is that this bull was dated the twelfth of August which was approximately eight days before the hearing at Chinon took place. This can be explained by the fact that the papal notaries were accustomed to backdate any important document from the end of the month when it was received by King Philip. At this stage he could no further interfere with the outcome.

With all this subterfuge, it remains a mystery why the pope, some four years later, dissolved the Order of the Temple.

BIBLIOGRAPHY

Addison, C.G. *The History of the Knights Templar*. Longman.

Barber, M. ed. *The Military Orders.*

Barber, M. *The Origins of the Order of the Temple*. Studia Monastica XII.

Baigent, Michael & Liegh, Richard. *The Templars and the Lodge*. 1991. pp101-110.

Baigent, Michael L & Liegh, Richard. *The Holy Blood and the Holy Grail*. London.

Bothwell-Gosse, A. *The Templars*. London.

Brewer, J. S. ed. *Giraldi Cambrensis Opera*. London.

Brown, D. *The Da Vinci Code*. London.

Burnes, J. *A Sketch of the History of the Knights Templar*. Edinburgh.

Campbell, G.A. *The Knights Templar, Their Rise and Fall*.London.

Coggereshall, Ralph. *Chronicum Anglicorum.*

Cooper, A. ed. *A New History of Ireland*. Vol.II. Oxford.

Dermot, B. *The Knights Templar in County Louth*. Seanchas Ardmacha (4)

Ebden, E.P. ed. *Great Role of the Pipe*. London.

Fanthorpe, L. & P. *The Secrets of Rennes-le-Chateau*. London.

Forey, A. *The Military Orders: From the 12th to the Early 14th Centuries.*

Forey, A. *Women and the Military Orders in the 12th,13th,14th Centuries.*

Frale, B. *The Chinon Chart: Papal Absolution to the Last Templar.* Journal of Medieval History 30 (2004).

Hore, P.H. *History of the Town and County of Waterford.* London.

Laidler, K. *The Head of God: Lost Treasure of the Templars.* London.

Larking, L.B. *The Knights Hospitallers in England.* 1338 Inquest.

Leclerq, J. & Rochais, H.M. eds. *Bernard of Clairvaux. De Laude Novae Militae.* V.111.

Leask, H.C. *Irish Churches and Monastic Buildings.* Dundalk.

MacInerny, Rev. M.O.P. *Templars in Ireland.* Vol.II.July/Dec. Irish Ecc. Review.

MacNiocaill, Ph.D. *Documents relating to the Suppression of the Templars in Ireland.* Analecta Hibernica. Vol.24.

Martin, E. *The Trials of the Templars.* London.

Nicholson, H. *Templars, Hospitallers and Teutonic Knights.* Leicester.

Perkins, C. *The Knights Templar in the British Isles.* Eng. Hist. Review.25.1910/p215.

Smith, B. *Colonisation and Conquest in Medieval Ireland.* Cambridge.

Upton-Ward, J.M. *The Rule of the Templars: The French Text.*

Wilkins, *Concilia.*

William of Tyre, *A History of Deeds Done Beyond the Sea.* Trans. Babcock, E.A.

Wilson, I. *The Blood and the Shroud.* London.

Wood, Herbert. *The Templars in Ireland.* Proceedings of the Royal Irish Acad..26.

SOURCES WITH REFERENCE TO IRELAND

These references deal with certain locations and sites in Ireland where Templar Properties are recorded to have existed especially those transferred to the Knights Hospitallers after the dissolution of the Order of the Templars.

Abbreviated.

A M. Archdall, *Monasticum Hibernicum*
AI. Annals of Ireland by Friar Clyn
A4M. Annals of the Four Masters. Ed. John O'Donovan
AH. Analecta Hibernica. (IMC)
AM. Annals of Munster
Arch.Hib. Archivium Hibernicum
Arch.J. Archaeological Journal
BBL. Black Book of Limerick
J.Beg. Begley, J. The Diocese of Limerick
BM. British Museum
Cassells Gazetteer of Great Britain and Ireland
Cogan. The Diocese of Meath
Cork.A.S. Cork Historical and Archaeological Society
CS. Chronicum Scotorum
F. Falkiner, Litton, C. *The Hospital of Saint John of Jerusalem in Ireland*
H. Hogan, E. S.J. *Onomasticon Goedelicum*. R.I.A.
Hore. Hore. P. H. *History of the Towns and County of Wexford*
IER. Irish Ecclest. Records
IHS. Irish Historical Studies
Joyce. Joyce, P.W. Irish Place Names
Lenihan. Lenihan, M. Limerick, its Hist and Antiq.
Lewis. Lewis, S. Topographical Dictionary of Ireland
L.Leinst. Book of Leinster

MG. Mac Geoghegan. Abbe. History of Ireland.

NLI. National Library of Ireland.

Orpen. Orpen, G. H. Ireland under the Normans.

OS. Ordinance Survey Maps.

PRJ. Calendar of Patent Rolls 1-16.

PROI. Public Record Office of Ireland.

R.H.S. Royal Historical Society.

RSAI. Journal, Royal Society of Antiquaries of Ireland.

Ryan. Ryan, J., S. J. Irish Monasticism, Origins and Dev.

Smith. Smith, C. The County and City of Cork.

Smith K. Smith, C. The County of Kerry.

Smith.W. Smith, C. The County and City of Waterford.

U Usher, J. Antiquities Eccles. Britannicarum.

INDEX

Odo of Saint-Armand, 49
Omni datum optimum, 25
Order of Teutonic Knights, 23, 26, 154, 166
Ottoman Turks, 192

Palestine, 12, 74, 92
Papacy, 22, 40, 50, 75, 78, 156, 197, 198
Paris Temple, 17, 54, 194
Peter of Bologna, 150
Philip IV. King of France, 17, 75, 77, 145, 146, 152, 153, 156, 163, 169
Pilgrims, 12, 13, 15, 19, 20, 22, 23, 25, 28, 41, 48, 49, 52, 54, 56, 57, 70, 195
Portugal, 51, 160, 161, 164, 165, 178
Preceptories, 16, 32, 42, 43, 45-48, 50, 81, 82, 84, 86, 87, 100-102, 136, 140, 155, 156, 158, 167, 173, 175, 179, 198

Relics, 45, 65, 72, 78, 153, 154, 156, 194
Rhodes, 56, 212
Richard the Lionhearted, 15, 53, 57, 67-71, 193, 212
Rochelle, la, 60, 196
Robert de Craon, Grand Master, 28, 213
Rome, 13, 15, 17, 24, 40, 52, 75, 162, 193
Rosslyn, 168, 188, 189, 190, 191
Rule of Life, 9, 13, 20, 24, 33, 34, 39, 45, 46, 48, 77, 78, 88, 154, 160, 189, 195

Safed, 65
Saladin, 15, 17, 61-63, 65, 68-71, 193
Santiago – Order of, 160
Saphet, 31
Saracens, 15, 162, 179, 202
Secrecy, 17, 54, 101, 116, 146, 157, 171
Seljuk Turks, 19,68
Shipping, 53, 56, 60
Sligo, County, 16, 82, 107, 139, 172
Sorcery, 77
Spain, 14, 17, 31, 42, 46-48, 52, 75, 78, 93, 153, 160, 162-164

Temple House, 101, 107, 139
Temple Mount, 21, 23
Temple of Solomon, 13, 21, 28, 35, 187, 189, 194
Tipperary, County, 102, 137, 138
Tripoli, 58, 61, 63, 66
True Cross, 38, 156, 193, 194

Urban II. Pope, 19

Vienne, Council of, 7, 150, 153, 182, 202

Walter Map, 53
Waterford, 16, 60, 81, 88, 90, 91, 103-105, 138-142, 181
Wealth, 13, 17, 31, 32, 53, 74, 76, 77, 153, 174, 195, 197
Wexford, 16, 81, 103, 104, 142, 143, 184
William of Tyre, 13, 15

Also available by the same author

THE CASTLES OF COUNTY LIMERICK

ISBN 0 95194159 3

A studiously researched reference to the medieval history of Limerick and the castles built between 1200 and 1700 CE. An introduction setting the historical context is followed by over 140 individual entries detailing the position, remains and history of each castle. Some of the more colourful legends are also recalled. Contains colour photographs, pen and wash drawings, plans and map.

THE CASTLES AND FORTIFIED HOUSES OF WEST CORK

ISBN 0 951 94158 5

An indispensable reference to the history of West Cork from 1150 to 1700 with details of the history and legends surrounding the castles of the region. With individual entries for 110 castles, line drawings by Martin Law and map.

THE CASTLES OF THE KINGDOM OF KERRY

ISBN 0 95194155 0

A fascinating look into the history of Kerry and Desmond between 1190 and 1700. A substantial historical introduction is followed by over 100 entries accompanied by colour photographs, black and white drawings and maps.

March into Oblivion

ISBN 0 95194154 2

A fictionalised retelling of the events after the battle of Kinsale in 1602 when Donal Cam O'Sullivan Bere lead his followers on the epic march from Glengarriff to Leitrim.

Sive O'Leary

ISBN 0 95194157 7

An historical novel of epic scale set at the time of the land wars in rural Ireland at the end of the eighteenth century.

Where the Deer Ran Wild

ISBN 0 95194151 8

A collection of reminiscences and stories based in and around the author's home area of Bantry and Bantry Bay.